Elegant Etiquette in the Nineteenth Century

Elegant Etiquette in the Nineteenth Century

Mallory James

PEN & SWORD
HISTORY

First published in Great Britain in 2017 by
PEN AND SWORD HISTORY
an imprint of
Pen and Sword Books Ltd
47 Church Street, Barnsley, South Yorkshire S70 2AS

ISBN 978 1 52670 520 4

Printed and bound in England
by CPI Group (UK) Ltd, Croydon, CR0 4YY

Typeset in Times New Roman by
CHIC GRAPHICS

Pen & Sword Books Ltd incorporates the imprints of Pen & Sword
Airworld, Archaeology, Atlas, Aviation, Battleground, Discovery,
Family History, Fiction, History, Maritime, Military, Military Classics,
Politics, Select, Social History, True Crime, Frontline Books,
Leo Cooper, Remember When, Seaforth Publishing, The Praetorian
Press, Wharncliffe Local History, Wharncliffe Transport.
Wharncliffe True Crime and White Owl.

For a complete list of Pen and Sword titles please contact
Pen and Sword Books Limited
47 Church Street, Barnsley, South Yorkshire, S70 2AS, England
E-mail: enquiries@pen-and-sword.co.uk
Website: www.pen-and-sword.co.uk

Contents

List of Plates

6. Fashion plate (promenade dress) by Rudolph Ackermann, London, England, 1 December 1816. Costume and Textiles Department, The Los Angeles County Museum of Art; retrieved from http://collections.lacma.org/node/247656; gift of Charles LeMaire. Image believed to be in the public domain.

7. Woman's bag (reticule), England, *c.* 1840. Costume and Textiles Department, The Los Angeles County Museum of Art; retrieved from http://collections.lacma.org/node/214049; purchased with funds provided by Suzanne A. Saperstein and Michael and Ellen Michelson, with additional funding from the Costume Council, the Edgerton Foundation, Gail and Gerald Oppenheimer, Maureen H. Shapiro, Grace Tsao and Lenore and Richard Wayne. Image believed to be in the public domain.

8. Fashion plate (walking dress) by Rudolph Ackermann, London, England, June 1814. Costume and Textiles Department, The Los Angeles County Museum of Art; retrieved from http://collections.lacma.org/node/252738; gift of Dr and Mrs Gerald Labiner. Image believed to be in the public domain.

9. Woman's bonnet, England or United States, late 1850s. Costume and Textiles Department, The Los Angeles County Museum of Art; retrieved from http://collections.lacma.org/node/233864; gift of the Pasadena Art Museum. Image believed to be in the public domain.

10. Fashion plate (walking dress) by Rudolph Ackermann, London, England, August 1814. Costume and Textiles Department, The Los Angeles County Museum of Art; retrieved from http://collections.lacma.org/node/252755; gift of Dr and Mrs Gerald Labiner. Image believed to be in the public domain.

11. Woman's parasol, Europe, *c.* 1865. Costume and Textiles Department, The Los Angeles County Museum of Art; retrieved from http://collections.lacma.org/node/213955; purchased with funds provided by Suzanne A. Saperstein and Michael and Ellen Michelson, with additional funding from the Costume Council, the Edgerton Foundation, Gail and Gerald Oppenheimer, Maureen H. Shapiro, Grace Tsao and Lenore and Richard Wayne. Image believed to be in the public domain.

LIST OF PLATES

Please note, it cannot be guaranteed that links will function and responsibility cannot be taken for the content of links and websites. Thank you for your understanding.

An Introductory Note

There is something about etiquette which makes one, on occasion, want to shy away from it. It does feel rather riskily snobbish and rather worryingly pretentious. Or at least, it is easy to worry that other people might perceive etiquette in that way. And so, sometimes, it makes a person want to jump back and declare, 'Who? Me? Talking about etiquette? Oh no, absolutely not. I'm not that sort of person at all!'

Well, let us take a moment to raise a white flag for the too-easily maligned topic of etiquette. Of course, it could be made into a metaphorical stick of snobbery and pretension with which to beat other people. But that would not be a very nice thing to do at all. Indeed, it would be deeply unpleasant. Etiquette, as it is understood here, is not about snobbery or pretension. Instead, it is about looking at what it means to be polite. Or, more specifically in relation to this book, it is about looking at what it meant to be polite in the nineteenth century. This entails exploring, and of course attempting to answer, a number of questions. What did a lady or gentleman have to know in order to be polite? What did they have to do? What did they have to say? What behaviour was or was not expected of them? What conduct was and was not acceptable? To be brief, what did people have to do to get things right? In terms of understanding politeness, we are interested in the actions and behaviours which were thought to be proper, respectable and indicative of good conduct.

Thus, this history of etiquette is not about looking at ways in which people could be mean in the nineteenth century. Instead, it is about uncovering ways in which people were able to be nice. Of course, we can (and will) make witty remarks about vulgarity and ill-breeding in relation to breaches of etiquette. It is so easily done that it cannot really be helped. And if that makes people smile wryly, then it is probably no bad thing. This is meant to be a fun history book, after all. But the point stands that the interest is in politeness, not pretension.

AN INTRODUCTORY NOTE

Further to understanding what it meant to be polite, and how people went about being polite, delving into etiquette allows us to try and picture the world of the nineteenth century. It enables us to contemplate the lives and experiences of the ladies and gentlemen during that period. It is a means by which we might steal a glimpse – as though through a gap between two curtains – and see how they might have lived. Etiquette provides an insight into habits and customs which shaped daily life, such as paying calls and going to balls. It also serves as a way to consider how people went about their lives. So, for example, how a lady or gentleman might have eaten their dinner or how they might have sealed a letter. This will also enable us to contemplate the physical objects which were linked to matters of etiquette and which would have been part of the daily lives of ladies and gentlemen. In the case of letters this would mean things such as paper, ink and sealing wax. This physical aspect should lend further depth to the picture we are trying to paint.

These matters, and more, will be explored over the course of the following chapters. The aim is to create a guide to the history of etiquette in the nineteenth century. It will explore things a lady or gentleman might have known and done, so that they could go about their business without leaving a trail of slights, insults and offences in their wake. In short, it will explore how they would have got through life without offending absolutely everyone. And, as mentioned above, we will be able to consider the experience of daily life at the same time.

However, even though we have now agreed that etiquette is a perfectly un-snobbish topic of investigation, there are some additional points which must be questioned before we can proceed any further with our jaunt back into the nineteenth-century world.

Firstly, one aspect which must be considered are the terms 'lady' and 'gentleman'. The nineteenth century was a period of growth for those people who, in the course of this era, became known as the middle class. For the purposes of our exploration of etiquette, where the terms 'lady' or 'gentleman' are used, they shall be meant in a self-selecting spirit, i.e. on the basis that people chose for themselves whether they were ladies or gentlemen. Consequently, no set or specific criteria beyond personal interpretation is attached to the terms. This is because such a stance is felt to be in keeping with the context of nineteenth-century etiquette manuals – from which much of the research for this book has been drawn – as they can be viewed as a means of self-improvement and social advancement. Generally speaking, etiquette manuals were not aimed at people established in their social position, or at the old aristocratic and gentry families. Instead, they were aimed at the newly arrived middle class. As a result, any stance other than the one taken seems rather mean-spirited. Indeed, to take any other would be distinctly odd, given all that has just been said about how this is a history of politeness, not rudeness.

Secondly, in using etiquette manuals to tell us about customs and behaviours in the nineteenth century, we have to be aware of what they cannot tell us. Etiquette manuals have to be read as books containing advice and suggestions. They were a guide to, and an explanation of, how a lady or gentleman was supposed to behave and the things they were supposed to do. Ladies and gentlemen were under no obligation to follow their instructions. There was nothing stopping them from flouting conventions or ignoring the rules. It might have been to their benefit to follow what we might consider 'best practice', but that does not mean that they did. Thus, we cannot say that everyone behaved in a certain way, or did a certain thing. Simply put, we cannot talk about etiquette or behaviour in absolute terms. To put this into context, we cannot talk about behaviour in absolute terms even now. What one person considers polite, another person considers rude. What one person considers absolutely necessary, another person considers a waste of time. We have to extend this nuance to our reading of history.

In consequence, we must be circumspect when talking about a period of time or a group of people as a whole. Whilst it would be very interesting to do so, it is not really possible to capture or re-create the full experience of life for ladies and gentlemen in the nineteenth century. Unless we can travel back in time and live a new life from start to finish, we will never really know what it was like to think or feel whilst living in a world that is so very different from our own. And even if we could do that, it would still only be the experience of one life. It would not be an experience of everyone else's life as well. After all, ladies and gentlemen of that period, as the people of any other, were individuals. As such, their lives were unique to them. Further to this and in terms of our own ability to imagine the past, it is one question – for example – to ask what would it be like to never hear or see a modern television again. It is an entirely different question to ask what it would be like to see one for the first time, and to have little or no understanding of the technology behind it. How do we know how any nineteenth-century lady or gentleman, yet alone all of them, would respond to such a sight? In attempting to imagine the past, we must recognise that the picture we paint will have been faded and blurred by the intervening years.

In addition, by talking about the lives of ladies and gentlemen, it is important to take a moment to recall that this means we are talking about a particular set of people in the nineteenth century. The etiquette of drawing rooms, dining rooms and ballrooms was far removed from the experience many people had of life in that period. Consequently, this history of etiquette is not an exhaustive history of nineteenth-century life. After all, how to eat a piece of fish properly was unlikely to have bothered someone who was more concerned with how to get that piece of fish, or any food at all, on to their plate to start with. Also, even when just talking about ladies and gentlemen, we have to bear in mind that this could refer to some very different styles of life. A duke in his stately home was a gentleman, but so was a vicar in his vicarage.

Furthermore, the nineteenth century was a period of significant change. This was the era which started with the Georgians and ended with the Victorians. It was the period which saw the continued development of the Industrial Revolution. The examples could go on. This century of change means that a lady or gentleman in 1800 would have lived in a very different world to a lady or gentleman in 1900. This must also be taken into account with regard to etiquette. Thus, this book shall try to consider particular changes in advice given across the century, and to situate etiquette hints within the wider time span of the century.

Nevertheless, we shall seriously endeavour to try and bring some part of the nineteenth-century world back to life for the modern reader. This book is an attempt to comprehend what it might have been like to walk down a street in London more than a hundred years ago, or to sit at a dining table, or to dance in a ballroom. In spite of the restrictions, which we must in all fairness acknowledge, exploring the etiquette of the nineteenth century begins to open up a door for that attempt. Etiquette can be used as a medium through which to examine the norms, customs, expectations and pressures which permeated daily life. It highlights habits and customs and – simply put – things which were central to ladies' and gentlemen's experiences. Calling cards were something they touched. Frock coats were something they wore. The quadrille was something they danced. A carriage was something they travelled in. The order of precedence was something they observed. An introduction was something to be properly made. In short, and in spite of all the limitations the passage of time has placed upon us, we can press our ears to the door, squint through the keyhole, push it open a crack, and try to see that world again in the best way we can and to the best of our understanding.

CHAPTER ONE

A Thorough Consideration of Rank, Precedence and the Application of Titles

Rank and precedence were central to the social world of nineteenth-century ladies and gentlemen. Understanding and acknowledging rank and precedence was, in many ways, the basis of etiquette. If the rules of etiquette were followed so that people could be polite to each other, then showing deference to rank and acknowledging one's place in the order of precedence were central tenets of politeness.

The subjects of rank and precedence occurred repeatedly in relation to matters of etiquette. They influenced speech, the formation of acquaintances, and even the process by which a lady or gentleman went into dinner. As they were so central to nineteenth-century life, rank and precedence are the first subjects with which we shall grapple. To begin, we shall consider the framework of rank in the nineteenth century, and explore the social make-up of the world in which ladies and gentlemen moved. However, it was not enough for a lady or gentleman to simply know about rank. Rank had to be demonstrated. Therefore, we must also question what it meant to give or take precedence. A final point to consider, which was closely bound up with rank and precedence, was the use and application of titles. How people addressed one another was often influenced by considerations of rank and precedence, and was naturally an important aspect of etiquette.

On the face of it, understanding rank and precedence in the nineteenth-century world seems fairly straightforward. At the top of the social pile there was, of course, the monarch. Their royal relations came next, followed by the aristocracy. Then the gentry took their place in the social order. The gentry were in turn followed by those of

1

a rather awkward social stratum. These were the people who became known as the middle class, or the middle classes. Those at the top of this category included people such as financiers, lawyers and generally those who were wealthy. Then, in the same category, but of lesser consideration, were people such as less-successful merchants and lower ranking clergymen. From there, the social framework deepened and widened to encompass those such as servants and labourers. It left the very poorest at the very bottom.

Yet, whilst this is, broadly speaking, a fair enough outline of the nineteenth-century social ladder, it would clearly make etiquette far too simple if that was the end of it. It is only the beginning. In order to understand the social world within which ladies and gentlemen lived, we have to understand the circles in which they mixed or may have aspired to mix. Therefore, the structure of both the aristocracy and gentry are of particular relevance to our exploration of etiquette and nineteenth-century life. So, we shall delve into them in more detail.

To start, the aristocracy, by which is meant peers and their families, had their own ranks and distinctions. A lady or gentleman might have been a member of the aristocracy – which, to be fair, did suggest that they were doing quite well in the social pecking order – but that did not mean that they were at the top, or that they were excused from deferring to those of higher rank. The aristocratic peerage had its own hierarchy of titles: duke, marquis, earl, viscount and baron. The female counterparts of these titles were as follows: duchess, marchioness, countess, viscountess and baroness. Of course, it must be pointed out that whilst the past tense is used here in relation to the nineteenth century, these titles and ranks are clearly still in use today. However, to return to the matter at hand, although two gentlemen might both have been members of the aristocracy, if one was an earl and the other a baron, the former would have ranked higher within the peerage than the latter.

It would have been advantageous for a lady or gentleman – particularly if they moved, or had aspirations to move, in elevated social circles – to understand how titles were constructed. Let us start at the top, with the example of a duke. His title would have been constructed as the Duke of Somewhere. So that no inhabitants of any place or county and no bearers of any names feel slighted, we shall simply assume that all the lords and ladies of the following examples are the lords and ladies of an unspecified 'somewhere' or 'something'. It would be really quite regrettable to give offence so early on in the book, after all.

Marquises and earls often formed their titles after a similar fashion to dukes. For instance, an earl's title could have been constructed as the Earl of Somewhere. Correspondingly, his wife's title would have been the Countess of Somewhere. A viscount normally had the 'of' omitted. So, whilst his title may have been the Viscount of Somewhere, it would usually have been constructed as Viscount Something. Similarly, a baron would have been titled as Baron Something. However, this form of his title would rarely have been used, and he would generally have been known as Lord Something.

After the ranks of the peerage, there were two further, titled ranks which were bestowed upon commoners. These were known as baronetcies and knighthoods, and those who held these ranks were generally considered to be members of the gentry. Whilst gentlemen holding these ranks would have been addressed in the same way, only a baronet could pass his title onto the next generation. Thus, a baronetcy ranked higher, and normally carried more prestige, than a knighthood. A baronet could have inherited a title going back generations. If his pedigree was as old as the hills he owned, he was unlikely to find that people turned their nose up at his acquaintance. Indeed, the same could be said for a great landowner from an old, untitled family. A knighthood, in contrast, might have been granted to a gentleman whose only distinction was the hard work of having recently made a fortune in trade. And there were certain ladies and gentlemen who chose to avoid others who still smelled of shop, as they might have chosen to phrase it.

Baronets and knights would have been known by their title, 'Sir', followed by their first name and surname. When addressed in conversation, they would have been called 'Sir' followed by their first name only. The wife of a baronet or knight was addressed, and referred to, as 'Lady', followed by her husband's surname. Naturally, this will be dealt with in more detail later on in this chapter, when we focus on the application of titles and forms of address.

However, escaping the realms of the noble and titled did not guarantee an escape from the issue of rank. After all, a lady or gentleman did not need to be in possession of a title in order to belong to the gentry. Indeed, even being engaged in a profession did not preclude a gentleman and his family from entry. Of course, owning an estate and not needing to work for a living were good indicators of higher ranking social status. Yet, being entitled to presentation at court was another mark of social status, and this honour was conferred upon certain professions. Also, to actually be engaged in trade directly, i.e. to take direct payment for your goods or services, was often a mark of a lower social rank.

In 1870 *Mixing in Society* defined military and naval officers, members of the clergy and physicians as people engaged in aristocratic professions, which also conferred the honour of presentation at court to wives and daughters. Lesser ranking professions, which meant that presentation was not possible, included general practitioners of medicine, merchants and any other men of business, with the exception of bankers. In the following decade, *Etiquette: What to Do and How to Do It* declared that clergymen, military and naval officers, barristers, medical professionals, leading bankers, merchants, artists and, in short, anyone who was extremely wealthy could be counted amongst the ranks of the gentry. Towards the close of the nineteenth century, *Manners and Rules of Good Society* echoed this definition.

As discussed at the beginning of this chapter, some of these professions were also linked to the middle classes. However, the lines between the various gradations of social status would most likely – at least in some cases – have been more blurred than clear-cut. For example, two gentlemen might have pursued a career in law. One might have come from a family of no particular note, whilst another might have been a younger son of an old, distinguished and landed family who had the benefit of some kindly patrons. That one might have fallen more into the ranks of the middle class, and the other amongst the gentry, is not inconceivable.

Of course, it was not enough for a lady or gentleman simply to understand the hierarchy of peerage or which professions allowed a person to be counted amongst the gentry. These things conferred rank, and rank conferred precedence. Precedence was an integral aspect of nineteenth-century etiquette. Giving or taking precedence was a reflection of rank. A person of higher rank would have taken precedence over a person of lower rank, whilst the person of lower rank would have given precedence to a person of higher rank.

We have already mentioned this in relation to earls and barons. Whilst both an earl and a baron would have been members of the peerage, an earl would have ranked higher in the order of precedence. The order of precedence was essentially a framework of who should come first. A clear example of the order of precedence in action was the process by which a lady or gentleman went into dinner. If our hypothetical earl and baron went to the same dinner, the earl would have gone into the dining room ahead of the baron. Acknowledging rank and precedence was polite, ignoring them was rude.

However, before we proceed any further with this aspect of etiquette, it is important to stress that although two people might have been of different ranks, that one person might have had to give precedence to another did not in any way diminish their claim to being a lady or a gentleman. It was, in fact, the opposite case. In the early years of the nineteenth century, James Ansell contended in *Principles of Politeness* that a true gentleman would always show the required respect for his superiors, but that this respect would have been characterised by the ease and grace of a man secure in his own position. *The Mirror of Graces* stressed that elegant women knew and took their place in the order of precedence with decorum, and that those who sought to push ahead or start ballroom disputes over who went where displayed a sort of vulgarity with which no sensible person would have wanted to be associated.

For instance, we would probably think that someone was being rude if they pushed ahead of us in a supermarket queue. Making comparisons across time and space is always a rather dubious undertaking, but demanding to go higher in the order of precedence for dinner – especially when the claim to this privilege was mistaken, false or tenuous – could be understood in a fairly similar fashion. It essentially meant that a lady or gentleman was pushing in, or pushing ahead, and that does tend to put other people's noses out of joint. Of course, one difference in the comparisons is that, in a busy supermarket queue, the offender and offended are unlikely to meet again. If two people had been invited to the same dinner party, the chance of their paths crossing in the future was probably higher. Furthermore, having someone push in front in a queue in the modern world is generally nothing more than an inconvenience and annoyance. It is not an affront to rank or precedence, or the established social hierarchy in which we live. It should perhaps be added then, that the nineteenth-century example of offence carries rather more weight than the twenty-first-century one. It was given more to illustrate a context or situation, rather than to serve as a direct comparison.

Yet precedence influenced more than just the order in which people went from the drawing room to the dining room. It was a central factor to many questions of etiquette and many social interactions. It will be a recurring theme in the chapters which follow. And, of course, the etiquette of getting from the drawing room to the dining room naturally warrants far more consideration than it has received here. But we shall address that want of attention in due course.

Nevertheless, whilst the framework of rank and precedence considered so far has been rather clear-cut, this was not always the case. If we return to the example of our earl and baron, it is quite simple to say that an earl came higher in the peerage than a baron. But what if there were two earls? Within the ennobled ranks, there was not only a distinction of rank attached to each title, but also to the longevity of that title in relation to other holders of the same title. Whilst two gentlemen might both have been an earl, it would have been the earl whose peerage was created first who would have held the higher precedence. Thus, it is important to note that a young earl might have taken precedence over an earl far senior to him in years.

CHAPTER ONE

A further example of a precedence conundrum might have been posed by the daughter of a peer, baronet or knight. If she had married a commoner, she would have kept her own rank in the order of precedence. If she had married a peer, she would have taken his rank.

As well as this, we must bear in mind that precedence still had to be considered even when there were no titles. Where all other factors of social position were generally equal, then a married person would have been given precedence over an unmarried person, or an older person over a younger one.

Even within an individual family, the issue of precedence still permeated social interaction. For instance, the eldest daughter of a family would have taken precedence over her younger sisters. Thus, when getting into a carriage, an elder sister would have been given a better seat before her younger sister.[1] And when going into dinner, she would have gone first.[2]

Simply put, precedence was a decisive factor in shaping how people went about being polite. A willingness to give precedence was a demonstration of civility by ladies and gentlemen. Not giving precedence suggested rudeness. After all, if the daughter of a baronet was entitled to go into dinner before the daughter of a commoner, and the latter knew that and created some sort of situation whereby she went first, well, perhaps we shall simply say that it may not have been the most genteel thing for her to have done. Again, and in reflection of the centrality of precedence to daily life, if the younger daughter of a family jumped up into the carriage first and took a better seat, it would not have been a particularly courteous way to behave towards her elder sister.

Regarding the etiquette of rank and precedence, the next matter to consider is the application of titles in speech and forms of address. The way in which a person was addressed could reflect their social position and could also indicate the social position of the person who spoke to them. More generally, even when there were no titles of rank to consider, a lady or gentleman would have needed to know how to address someone properly and thus politely.

Therefore, if we begin at the very top of the nineteenth-century social ladder, we must start with the form of address which was applied to the monarch. The monarch was 'Your Majesty' whilst their spouse, children and siblings were 'Your Royal Highness'. However, according to advice from the second half of the century, 'Your Majesty' was the form used by those belonging to the middle class and anyone below that class in rank. Those belonging to the aristocracy or gentry would have addressed the monarch, who by that point was of course Queen Victoria, as 'Ma'am'.

According to the same advice, a duke and duchess would have been colloquially addressed as 'Duke' and 'Duchess' when in the company of their own people, which we might generally take to mean the upper classes of society. All other people would have addressed them as 'Your Grace'.

We shall now begin to find examples rather helpful for illustrating forms of address. However, as we have no desire to favour any particular place or name, the hypothetical lords and ladies we imagine here shall all be Lord A and Lady A, and so on. After all, in a history of etiquette, it seems quite important to strenuously avoid all appearance of rudeness.

And so, to proceed swiftly onwards with the various ranks of the peerage, the form of address for a marquis and marchioness must come next. The upper classes would have addressed them as 'Lord A' and 'Lady A'. Everyone else would have addressed them as either 'My Lord' and 'My Lady', or as 'Your Lordship' and 'Your Ladyship'. In the same fashion, an earl and countess would have been 'Lord B' and 'Lady B' to the upper classes, and then 'My Lord', 'My Lady', 'Your Lordship' or 'Your Ladyship' to all other classes. Then, a viscount and viscountess would have been 'Lord C' and 'Lady C' amongst the upper classes, and would then have been addressed in the manner previously described by everyone else. These conventions also applied to barons and baronesses.

Another point about the application of titles which should be noted is that peeresses often addressed their husbands, or referred to them, by only the latter part of their title.[3] If the viscount and viscountess detailed above are taken as an example, then the viscount would have

CHAPTER ONE

been the Viscount C and addressed by the upper classes as Lord C. His wife, Lady C, could have spoken to him, or referred to him, as simply 'C' with perfect propriety.

Nevertheless, a caveat should be added here, which might have brought about a sigh of relief from many ladies and gentlemen in the nineteenth century. The excessive use of titles in conversation was frowned upon. Yes, ladies and gentlemen were meant to show deference to rank. No, they were not meant to go completely overboard about it. Only servants felt the need to, or were perhaps obliged to, use 'My Lord' and 'My Lady' as a form of punctuation when conversing with their superiors. A lady or gentleman should ideally have had the confidence to move amongst their superiors with dignity and ease, as well as deference.

Amongst the nobility, there was a further matter of etiquette to be taken into account. That matter was the use and application of courtesy titles. Courtesy titles were not proper titles, in the sense that they were not formal titles of the peerage. However, they were bestowed upon some family members of peers, namely their children and those children's spouses. Returning to what will be an oft-repeated theme in the rules of etiquette, these conventions were a means of conveying respect and politeness. In short, they were another polite delicacy that etiquette manuals advised ladies and gentlemen to master.

The eldest sons of dukes, marquises and earls were addressed as 'Lord' and were allowed to use one of their father's secondary titles – as a courtesy – until they inherited the main one. Thus, they would have been addressed as 'Lord D' by the upper classes, and as 'My Lord' or 'Your Lordship' by everyone else. Their wives would have been addressed in the corresponding fashion, either as 'Lady D', or as 'My Lady' or 'Your Ladyship'.

The younger sons of dukes and marquises were known as 'Lord' followed by their first name and surname. However, they would normally have been addressed in conversation as 'Lord' followed by their first name only. Their surname would only have been used in a letter, for example. Their wives would have been addressed in a corresponding style, thus as 'Lady' followed by their husband's first name. Outside of the upper classes, the younger sons of dukes and marquises would have been addressed as 'My Lord' or 'Your Lordship'. Their wives would have been addressed as 'My Lady' or 'Your Ladyship'.

The daughters of dukes, marquises and earls were styled as 'Lady' followed by their first name and surname. In conversation, they would have been addressed as 'Lady' followed by their first name only. However, those outside of the upper classes would have addressed them as 'My Lady' or 'Your Ladyship'. They would have retained this title and rank as long as they were unmarried, or if they married a commoner. If they married a peer, they would have taken his rank.

Let us say, for example, that Lady E (signifying her first name) was the daughter of an earl. She then married a commoner, who we shall call Mr F (denoting his surname). Rather than becoming Mrs F, she would have remained Lady E. Alternatively, let us suppose that Lady E married the eldest son of Viscount G instead. Perhaps she had decided that Mr F was not such a catch after all. In this instance, she would have remained Lady E whilst her husband held only a courtesy title. However, upon the death of her father-in-law, she would have become the new Viscountess G. This is because her husband would have become the new Viscount G, and would have held a title belonging to the peerage instead of a courtesy title. She would then have been addressed as Lady G (representing her husband's title) by the upper classes.

The younger sons of earls, and all children of viscounts and barons, were entitled to the prefix of 'the Honourable'. This was another courtesy title. However, the title 'the Honourable' would only have been used in writing and not in conversation. In conversation, those holding this title would simply have been 'Mr', 'Mrs' or 'Miss', depending upon which of these happened to be applicable.

Whilst it is all well and good to discuss how a lady or gentleman should have addressed peers and those with courtesy titles, it is also important to know the forms of address they would not have used. If a lady or gentleman wanted to be polite, avoiding mistakes was naturally a matter of some concern. One rule of particular note was that a title was not supposed to be abbreviated. For example, Lord Something, as we shall once again name him, should not have been addressed simply as Lord S. In the earlier years of the century, John Trusler warned in *A System of Etiquette* that it was never acceptable to do this, even if one were of equal or superior rank to the person with whom one spoke. However, this stance may have relaxed towards the end of the century. It was suggested that between close friends, of equal rank, such abbreviations could be permissible.[4]

After considering the application of titles with regard to peers and those possessing courtesy titles, the next group of people whose titles must be considered are baronets and knights. As mentioned previously, both a baronet and a knight would have been known as 'Sir' followed by their first name and surname. In conversation they would have been addressed as 'Sir' followed by their first name. Their surname would have been dropped, in this instance. In contrast, their wives would have been addressed as 'Lady' followed by their husband's surname. The wives of baronets and knights would also have been addressed as 'My Lady' or 'Your Ladyship' by those outside of the upper classes.

A further etiquette blunder, which a lady or gentleman would have been well-advised to avoid, would have been to address the wife of a knight or baronet by her husband's first name and surname. For example, we shall name a baronet Sir Robert Smith. Correctly, his wife should have been addressed as Lady Smith. If someone mistakenly addressed her as Lady Robert Smith, they would have no longer been using the form of address for the wife of a baronet, but would rather have been implying that she was the wife of the younger son of a duke or marquis.

However, even if we descend down the social ladder to those who were not in possession of ancient and lofty titles, there are still points of etiquette to consider in relation to the application of titles. In conversation, a lady or gentleman would have addressed someone as 'Mr', 'Mrs' or 'Miss' at all times. It was important that a lady or gentleman did not shorten someone's surname or drop their title. For instance, a gentleman was supposed be called 'Mr' followed by his surname. Thus, it would have been in very poor taste for someone to have addressed him as 'Mr' followed by only the first letter of his surname. Similarly, *Etiquette for Gentlemen* strongly discouraged its readers from simply addressing a gentleman by his surname alone. Yet, in the final decades of the century, it was said that abbreviating names and surnames was acceptable between very close friends of equal rank.[5]

Additionally, and in contrast to the etiquette which applied to peeresses, it would have been very improper for the wife of a commoner to refer to her husband by anything other than the full form of his address. He was Mr Smith or Mr Jones or whatever other surname belonged to him. It was felt rather vulgar for a wife to refer to her husband as 'Smith' or 'Mr J'.

The role of precedence within families also becomes apparent again in the use of the title 'Miss'. In a family with numerous daughters, the eldest would have been addressed as 'Miss' followed by her surname. Her younger sisters would have been called 'Miss' followed be either just their first names, or by both their first names and surname.

Professional occupation was another factor which influenced forms of address. *Manners and Rules of Good Society*, for example, advised its readers that an army officer should be addressed by his rank followed by his surname. However, whilst married women might have benefitted from a presentation at court due to their husband's profession, they did not take on any professional titles he might have had. To demonstrate this, if a gentleman held the rank of colonel, his wife would still have been addressed as 'Mrs' followed by his surname. She would not have been 'Mrs Colonel' followed by his surname. According to *Manners and Rules of Good Society*, a lady or gentleman would also have been in error if they addressed this hypothetical colonel as 'Colonel' – omitting his surname – unless they were a particularly close friend of his.

Further to this, it would have been very wrong for a lady or gentleman to have tried to avoid a person's title or form of address. To be brief, they were not supposed to refer to them in a roundabout sort of way. For instance, if a lady or gentleman wanted to ask after someone else's mother, father or other relation, they were supposed to refer to them by their proper title in the correct form.[6] This was thought to be more polite than simply asking about 'your sister', for example.

A final impropriety of note was the erroneous application of titles in referring to one's children as 'Master Peter' or 'Miss Catherine' or whatever the little darlings had been named.[7] It was felt that it was only appropriate to talk to servants in this way about any inhabitants of the family nursery.

Some Principal Points of Politeness
- A simple way of looking at the social hierarchy in the nineteenth century would be to lay it out in the following order: the royal family, the aristocracy, the gentry, the middle classes and then everyone else. The poorest in society came last.
- Rank and precedence shaped and determined customs of polite society, such as how people went into dinner.
- Additionally, rank and precedence influenced the forms of address which were used when people spoke to one another.
- Whilst it was polite to refer to the titled as 'My Lord' and 'My Lady' where appropriate, a lady or gentleman would not have done so too frequently.
- In general conversation amongst untitled people, ladies and gentle-man would have referred to each other as 'Mr', 'Mrs' and 'Miss' in most circumstances.
- Ladies and gentleman ran the risk of being thought impolite if they shortened names or dropped titles, unless they were on particularly intimate terms with the person in question.

CHAPTER TWO

The Weighty Matter of Good Company and Introductions

It was felt that a lady or gentleman should always have aimed to keep the very best company, or at least the very best company to which they could reasonably have aspired. The reason for this was found in self-improvement. If a lady or gentleman did not seek to improve themselves by associating with good company, then they risked falling into some sort of social decline through complacency and lack of effort.

However, the ladies and gentlemen of the nineteenth century would naturally have been obliged to temper their aspirations with a candid assessment of their own rank, location and general circumstances. To take a simple example, a young lady whose principal residence was a remote village, and whose parents preferred a retiring mode of life, could not have realistically expected to suddenly find herself in a London ballroom.

Hand in hand with this, a lady or gentleman was supposed to be discerning in their interpretation of what was called 'good company'. The longed-for London ballroom (at least, from the mind of our hypothetical young lady) might have been filled with glittering company, where she could dance all night, enjoy herself and generally be the all-round belle of the ball. Yet that did not necessarily mean that the assembled company was good company. The definition of good company was a theme which puzzled a number of etiquette manuals during the nineteenth century. One possible conclusion seems to have been that good company had as much to do with the internal character and substance of the ladies and gentlemen brought together, as with their respective ranks and social positions.

In *Principles of Politeness* from 1804, Ansell argued that good company was that which could be considered superior. But this superiority was not derived from birth, but rather from merit. Within this superiority of merit, Ansell felt that there were two distinct types of good company and that a gentleman ought to endeavour to keep both. Firstly, a gentleman was advised to keep fashionable good company, amongst people of birth and rank. Amongst such exalted personages, a gentleman would be able to learn the best possible manners. The second type of company to be sought was amongst gentlemen of learning and science, although Ansell warned that a gentleman should not allow himself to become too engrossed with such company. Such company was all well and good for a gentleman's intellect, but was not thought to be particularly useful in helping him to get on in the world.

In 1837, Arthur Freeling reiterated this point in similar terms in *The Pocket Book of Etiquette*. Good society, as defined in this example, was based upon birth, rank, respectability and fashion. A lady or gentleman would have found these things united in good society, and in such society wisdom, merit and the best possible manners would have been quite normal.

Similar advice was echoed later on in the century. In *Etiquette for All* from 1861, it was once more stressed that company had to be decent and respectable, in order for it to be good. Truly fashionable company entailed all of these things, but it was perfectly possible for a person of high rank to be lacking in some, what could perhaps be called, desirable fundamentals. High rank did not preclude a lady or gentleman from having low manners. The society of intellectuals was also encouraged, albeit on a limited basis. It was again felt that these lofty geniuses were too removed from daily life for constant immersion in their society to be beneficial to those with a merely average capacity for intellectual thought.

Thus, if our young lady had persuaded her retiring parents to allow her to attend a ball where there were people of fashion, superior social rank, meticulous propriety and where these attributes were ideally found united together, then she would have indeed succeeded in mixing in good company. However, if that ballroom had been filled with those of low birth and low conduct, then regardless of how many gentlemen asked her to dance or how much fun she had, the company could hardly have been considered good. Of course, we shall assume that in this hypothetical example, the young lady's parents would never have allowed her to attend a ball where such unseemly company was likely to be assembled.

However, just as ladies and gentlemen were warned to guard themselves against falling into improper forms of address in the previous chapter, equal fortitude was also needed to man the barricades against company which was not worthy of being kept. Indeed, we have already hinted at this. What could only, and most unfortunately, be deemed 'low company' was to be avoided at all costs.

Essentially, low company was the reverse of good company. Whilst good company might have raised a lady or gentleman up – both in a personal sense and in the eyes of the wider world – bad company would only have served to pull them down. Amongst low company, one would have found vulgar habits and manners. Vanity and folly might have led a person to stray into such company. A person stood a very good chance of feeling delightfully superior, after all, amongst the rude and the coarse. And there are few people who have never wanted to boost their egos now and again. But the short-lived pleasures were not worth the long-term losses. Vanity and folly might have tempted a gentleman to stray into such company, but those vanities would have been flattered and those follies encouraged by the sort of people he had degraded himself to mix with. And thus, once there, he could easily have been persuaded to stay. And the consequence, of what a gentleman might once have thought to be nothing more than a brief and harmless foray into low company, was ruin.

Gentlemen especially were warned against the vice and dissipation which awaited them if they kept the sort of company that led them to frequent taverns, brothels and gaming houses. Naturally, well-bred ladies did not need any warnings to avoid those particular haunts. Indeed, these particular warnings regarding low company could perhaps be seen to suggest that a greater opportunity for forming their own circle of acquaintance, without the supervision of an older and wiser chaperone, was available to young gentlemen.

Nevertheless, young ladies were encouraged to be prudent and circumspect in their conduct, and this can perhaps be seen as an extension of the dire warnings regarding the perils of low company. It was said that it was not possible for a lady to be too cautious with her reputation. Indeed, it was better for a lady to be thought ridiculous for her exacting sense of delicacy, than to risk being thought loose.[1]

This all brings us rather neatly on to the etiquette of introductions. The sense of selection and the importance thereof, which was demonstrated in the advice relating to good company, was echoed in the rules of etiquette which guided the process of introductions. Introductions are also an important matter of etiquette, and an important aspect of nineteenth-century life, to consider. Although a lady or gentleman might have aspired to mix in good company, nothing could have come of this aspiration if they had no circle of acquaintance and no prospect of making or receiving introductions.

Regarding the sense of caution just mentioned, ladies and gentlemen were urged to be careful in accepting offers of introduction. In the 1860s *Etiquette for All*, for instance, advised ladies and gentlemen to only accept the offer of an introduction if they completely trusted the acquaintance who made the offer. An introduction, once made, could not really be un-made. The inconvenience arising from an ill-judged introduction might have been slight. A lady or gentleman might have had the acquaintance of someone who was dull or a bit annoying forced upon them. However, there were far worse faults than dullness or annoyingness, and the dangers posed by low company could not be forgotten.

In addition, people who attempted, in the common way of speaking, to strike up an acquaintance were supposed to be viewed with suspicion.[2] If a true gentleman was desirous of an introduction, he would have sought to obtain one properly. He would not, in a coffee house or some other public place, have sought to subvert the established customs of proper etiquette.

However, a lady or gentleman did not just have to be vigilant when it came to receiving an introduction. The duty also fell upon them to be cautious when making, or offering to make, an introduction. After all, a lady or gentleman had a responsibility to polite society. They had to consider the interests of others, as well as their own. They were urged never to offer to make an introduction unless it was going to be desirable to all parties. Generally speaking, a lady or gentleman was supposed to obtain the permission of both people before performing an introduction. Indeed, this seems to have been advice which permeated throughout this period. *Hints on Etiquette* presented this as an important matter of politeness in 1836. *The Pocket Book of Etiquette* from 1837 laid it down as an absolute maxim of propriety. In 1840 *The Ladies Pocket Book of Etiquette* provided similar advice. It appeared again over forty years later in *Etiquette: What to Do and How to Do It*. And it appeared once more in *Manners for Men* in the final years of the century.

Whilst some alternative guidance was suggested – and as we mentioned before, we cannot assume that everyone felt the same way about something – prudent conduct was still advised. For example, it was suggested that it was more important to obtain prior permission when introducing gentlemen to ladies.[3] In that instance, the wishes of the lady always had to be consulted. However, when introducing two gentlemen to each other, permission did not always have to be sought. Nevertheless, the introduction should still only have been made when one was completely and absolutely sure the connection would be appreciated. Rank and precedence also came into play. It was suggested that as long as the lady or gentleman performing the introduction had consulted the person of superior rank, this gave them sufficient authority to make an introduction between two people.[4]

In short, when it came to making and receiving introductions, caution does seem to have been the order of the day, or perhaps the century.

However, even once a lady or gentleman had established that an introduction was permissible, and maybe even desirable, there was still plenty of potential for the whole thing to go disastrously wrong. There was no lack of advice put to ladies and gentlemen with regard to the best way for them to carry out an introduction.

To begin, which person of the two was introduced to the other person was very important. A principal component of good manners was that the person of lower rank was supposed to be introduced to the person of higher rank. However, ladies were the exception to this rule. They were always given precedence over gentlemen in the making of an introduction. It was a matter of polite courtesy. Therefore, regardless of other considerations of rank, a gentleman was always presented to a lady.

Let us suppose, for example, that Sir A was a baronet and Lord B was a viscount. In this instance, Sir A would have been introduced to Lord B. But, there was also a delightful young lady by the name of Miss C. Miss C, for the purposes of our example, was the daughter of an untitled commoner. He was, of course, perfectly gentlemanly and respectable. Despite being of a lower social position than both Sir A and Lord B, Miss C would not have been introduced to either of them. Instead, they would have been introduced to her.

Apparent equality of social rank did not necessarily make the task of introducing people any easier. After all, one person still had to be introduced to the other. If the two people were of equal social rank, then it was felt that the younger person should be introduced to the elder. Another way of determining the nature of the introduction was marital status. If two ladies were being introduced, and their rank was otherwise equal, then an unmarried lady would have been introduced to a married one. Of course, if the married lady was, for example, untitled, and the unmarried lady was the daughter of a marquis, then the married lady would have been introduced to her.

Next in the fraught process of introducing people was the way in which it was done. Once a lady or gentleman had determined which person should be presented to the other, they still had to translate that into polite conversation. According to advice given in the later decades of the century, the correct procedure was to introduce the first person to the second, and to do so succinctly and without repetition.[5] Thus, a lady or gentleman would have said something to the effect of, 'Miss Smith, Mrs Brown.' Or, for a further example, they might have said, 'Mrs Brown, Lady Jones.'

Both parties, thus introduced, would have had to acknowledge the performance of this little ceremony in some polite way. This was normally done with a bow. A handshake was permissible, but did not normally take place. A handshake would usually have been exchanged between those who shared a greater level of intimacy, which people who had only just been introduced could not have been expected to possess.

However, towards the end of the nineteenth century, *Manners and Rules of Good Society* detailed some instances in which the shaking of hands upon an introduction would have been perfectly acceptable or even expected. Hosts and hostesses were advised to shake hands with any stranger who was introduced to them in their own home. A lady engaged to be married was supposed to shake hands when she made the acquaintance of any relations of her future husband. Also, if two close friends of a lady or gentleman were introduced to each other by that lady or gentleman, it was felt fitting that they should shake hands.

In all of this, it was also important for ladies and gentlemen to be aware of times when an introduction should not be made. Indeed, there were a number of circumstances when a person might have been tempted to introduce people, assuming this was the polite thing to do, when they were, in truth, dreadfully mistaken. In those confusing circumstances, a lady or gentleman might have been in danger of breaching the rules of etiquette, in the mistaken belief that they were following them.

Take, for example, the following situation. A lady or gentleman might have been walking along with one very dear and agreeable friend, when they saw another, equally valued friend, approaching them. Well, what could have been more natural than to bring these two people together? Unfortunately, it was these well-meaning and kind-hearted thoughts that could easily have led to both cherished friends feeling put upon and offended. An introduction was an important matter. As previously discussed, it was something that should only have been done when the consent of the relevant parties had been obtained. The wishes of the lady or the person of superior rank had to be consulted, at least. Accordingly, if a lady or gentleman had only happened to chance upon the other friend whilst out and about, then it was best not to make an introduction in such circumstances.

Another similar situation was found in morning calls. Suppose again that two valued friends happened to pay a call at the same time, and were suddenly both together in a lady's home. Surely, this fortuitous occurrence was a sign that the two people should be introduced? What event could be happier? Once more, such kindly thoughts were in danger of leading our imaginary hostess into a breach of etiquette. Unacquainted morning callers were not supposed to be introduced to one another. If unacquainted people were present during the call, the best practice would have been for the hostess to address each caller in turn so that no one felt neglected, but for her also to ensure that the conversation did not become too general. The hostess should have only presumed to introduce the two people when she was sure that such an introduction would be acceptable to both parties, and that their respective social positions did not in some way pose a barrier to such an introduction being sprung upon them. Later advice suggested that an introduction in the above circumstances was more acceptable, but if the hostess felt it better to refrain for some reason, then she could do so with perfect propriety.[6] Instead, she would have spoken to the two parties in turn and not allowed the conversation to become too general, as mentioned above.

However, verbal introductions were not the only way of bringing two people together. It was also possible for a lady or gentleman to be introduced by a letter. An example of this might have been that a lady or gentleman was going to take up residence in a new place. If someone of the lady or gentleman's acquaintance knew a person who lived in that place, then they might have been kind enough to bestow upon the lady or gentleman in question a letter of introduction. The newly arrived lady or gentleman could then have passed the letter on to the established resident. Letters of introduction could smooth the path of a person's arrival in a new place and could help them to integrate into a new social circle. In short, a letter of introduction was a way of introducing two people, without the introducer having to be present.

Letters of introduction were thus matters of some delicacy. After all, it was no small thing to introduce two people to one another, as we have already discussed in some depth. Moreover, the success or failure of such an introduction (over which a lady or gentleman had no supervision or control after pen had been put to paper) might have had a lasting impact upon both acquaintances. We can imagine a number of ways in which this might have been the case. Both people might have looked rather unfavourably upon the introducer afterwards, if they had both found the company of the other distinctly disagreeable. Alternatively, it was not inconceivable that a lady or gentleman might have written a letter of introduction to a person who they had not seen for a number of years. The warmth of their friendship could have cooled with the passage of time, and the recipient might have resented the letter – and thus its writer – for foisting an unknown person upon their attention and goodwill.

In consequence, ladies and gentlemen were advised to consider a request to provide a letter of introduction as a deeply serious one. Indeed, if there was any doubt as to the reception with which the letter of introduction would be met, then it was thought better to decline the request than to risk causing any offence. If a lady or gentleman felt that it was necessary for them to decline to provide a letter of introduction, then it was suggested they should say they did not feel at liberty to provide one or something else to that effect.[7]

To provide some illustration for this matter of etiquette, let us suppose that there was a dashing young gentleman by the name of Mr D. Mr D had two friends – who we shall call Mr E and Mr F – and had applied to them both for a letter of introduction. Mr D had known Mr E for a long time and they were close friends. He had demonstrated to Mr E his estimable character and numerous admirable qualities many times. In contrast, Mr F was a relatively new acquaintance of Mr D, and they had only spoken to one another on a handful of occasions. Thus, whilst Mr E might have felt perfectly confident in providing Mr D with a letter of introduction, Mr F might have felt it more prudent for him to decline to provide such a letter. Perhaps Mr F did not feel he was at liberty to do so.

If a lady or gentleman decided, after careful consideration, that it was appropriate for them to provide a letter of introduction, there were certain niceties they would have been wise to observe. One especially noteworthy piece of advice was that it was best not to seal a letter of introduction. No one can pretend to be astonished that one person might have wanted to know what another person had written about them.

In the middle part of the century, *Etiquette, Social Ethics and the Courtesies of Society* drew attention to the reigning fashion for seals embossed with crests or the names of residences. Readers were advised to put letters of introduction into envelopes thus marked, and to request that their friend close the envelope themselves after they had read the contents. The importance of using good-quality notepaper was also stressed. Presumably, a lady or gentleman's best penmanship was also called for in such circumstances. After all, a letter of introduction was offered in lieu of a person's actual presence. It would therefore have been only natural to try and leave a good impression.

A lady or gentleman in possession of a letter of introduction, if they were interested in following the rules of etiquette, would have then endeavoured to present themselves and the letter to the intended reader with the utmost propriety.

At the start of the century, it was suggested that when a person had been supplied with a letter of introduction, they were honour-bound to deliver it in person and without delay.[8] However, later advice generally cautioned against suddenly appearing on a stranger's doorstep. Instead, it was thought preferable for a lady or gentleman to send the letter of introduction to the person in question, having enclosed one of their own calling cards alongside it. Simply turning up unannounced had the potential to be a rather awkward experience. It might have obliged the bearer to remain standing – watching the recipient read through the letter –whilst feeling as though the recipient was about to pass judgement upon their respectability. In contrast, sending the letter allowed the person receiving it to read it through in privacy and at their leisure.

The general pattern of conduct was that once the letter of introduction had been sent, the sender could have expected to receive a call from the recipient within the course of a few days. However, we can easily picture instances where this might not have been the case. The recipient might have been unwell, or the letter might have been a misjudgement and thus received as an impertinence. Or, the recipient might just have been feeling unfriendly and decided not to respond to the letter because of a turn of fancy.

Of course, it was one thing to be the bearer of the letter and consider that etiquette. The points mentioned above highlight that we must also consider the etiquette of the reverse situation, i.e. when a lady or gentleman had a letter of introduction sent to them. If a lady or gentleman received a letter of introduction, it was considered polite for them to acknowledge it in some way. To completely and utterly blank the receipt of such a letter was an offensive slight to both the bearer who had sent it, and the existing acquaintance who had written it for them.

Beyond that, what a lady or gentleman did in response to receiving the letter was another question. At the very least, a lady or gentleman ought to have left a card to acknowledge their receipt of the letter.[9] A lady or gentleman was not obligated to start extending dinner invitations, for example. Other advice suggested that a lady or gentleman really ought to actually pay a call and should try and bestow other acts of kindness on the bearer of the letter, such as escorting them to some local place of interest, attending a concert with them or, indeed, inviting them to dinner.[10]

It was also possible that a lady or gentleman might have received a letter of introduction in person, if the bearer was not acquainted with the established rules of etiquette. In those circumstances, if they recognised the handwriting of the person who wrote the letter of introduction, it was said that the best thing to do was to simply lay the letter to one side and start a conversation.[11] If a lady or gentleman could not immediately tell from the direction who of their acquaintance had written the letter, then they were advised to ask the bearer politely for permission to read it. Afterwards, once aware of the contents, they could act as they saw fit.

Some Principal Points of Politeness
- Ladies and gentlemen were advised to seek out good company and to avoid company which was bad.
- Good company had as much to do with good character, as it did to do with wealth and rank.
- Introductions were a delicate business. Generally speaking, it was best to get the permission of both people before introducing either of them to the other.
- When making an introduction, an inferior was always introduced to a superior.
- However, gentlemen were always introduced to ladies.
- Letters of introduction were also a matter of some importance. Deciding whether or not to provide a letter of introduction required careful consideration.
- A letter of introduction was not supposed to be sealed when it was given to the person who required it.
- It was thought better for the bearer of a letter of introduction to send it to the intended reader, rather than for them to deliver it in person.

CHAPTER THREE

Proper Conduct Whilst Out and About

Good manners were not supposed to be reserved for the very best of company. They were important in all situations. The rules of etiquette touched many aspects of daily life, including how a lady or gentleman was supposed to behave whilst out and about.

A lady or gentleman might have liked to imagine that a gaffe or faux pas committed amidst the hustle and bustle of a busy street went unnoticed. But, hidden amongst the crowd, there may well have been a witness. And it was not implausible that the offender and the witness might have met again at some later date, and that the first might then have been most unfortunately fixed in the mind of the second as ill-bred, ill-mannered and entirely unfit to mix in polite society. In consequence, etiquette manuals discussed what behaviour demonstrated good conduct and what behaviour was to be scrupulously avoided. Here, the recommended etiquette for how ladies and gentlemen were supposed to conduct themselves whilst on the street or whilst out walking for pleasure will be considered, along with other advice pertaining to travel in a carriage or by the new-fangled railway. New-fangled, of course, depending upon which part of the century a lady or gentleman happened to find themselves.

The first matter to consider is that the etiquette of the street actually began at home. It was important for a lady or gentleman to wear suitable clothing. After all, a lady or gentleman would have always sought to choose attire which was fitting to the occasion at hand. And there was attire which was, and which was not, fitting to be worn walking in the street. According to advice from the second half of the century, a lady would never have sought to draw attention to herself through her clothes when she was out and about. Thus, this would not have been the occasion for brightly coloured dresses, or anything else which might have been considered eye-catching. Towards the end of the century it was advised that a lady should carry a parasol in summer and a muff and umbrella in winter.[1] Presumably, she would then have been equipped to protect both her clothing and complexion.

Modest attire was also suggested for gentlemen, with darker coats preferable to lighter ones. In the 1830s, *The Pocket Book of Etiquette* also urged gentlemen to remember to wear the correct coat, by which was meant a frock coat rather than a dress coat. A frock coat was for the street, whilst a dress coat was for the drawing room. A gentleman carrying a cane was instructed, towards the close of the century, to hold it in the proper fashion. The advice in this instance was that the cane was supposed to be held at a 45 degree angle.[2]

The next matter of etiquette and behaviour to look at is the question of when a lady or gentleman went walking. We can presume that if a gentleman was engaged on a matter of business – if he had some important appointment to keep – or if a lady had some other pressing need to be out and about, then naturally those considerations would have dictated the timing of their excursion. However, if a lady or gentleman was walking for pleasure, then there were some hours during which it was considered more fashionable to be out and about than others. An example of walking for pleasure might have been to take a walk in a public park or promenade when in a town or watering place.

During the Regency period in the earlier part of the nineteenth century, for example, it was particularly fashionable to be seen in Hyde Park between the hours of 5 and 6 o'clock when the Season was underway. Of course, this meant not only walking, but riding and driving (in a carriage) as well. It was a chance for the well-bred and well-heeled to show themselves off to each other, and to anyone else who cared to watch them. The Season was the period of the year in which the upper classes descended upon London en masse. Simply put, it was their social season. Whilst there is some fluidity with the dates for the Season, it can broadly be said to have lasted from March until June.

According to *Etiquette: What to Do and How to Do It* from the 1880s, the fashionable hours for walking in London during the summer were between 12 o'clock and 2 o'clock. In the winter, the best time for walking was thought to be slightly later, between 2.30 and 4.30.

Naturally, the guidance on etiquette continued beyond advice on when it was a good time to be seen out and about. As has already been hinted at, reserve and propriety were matters a lady was supposed to take into account when out walking. One matter of etiquette of particular note was that of ladies walking alone.

According to advice given in the second half of the century, it would have been really quite improper for a young lady to walk alone in London. If the young lady in question was not old enough to be 'out' in society, then it was the role of her governess to accompany her when she went walking.[3] If she was 'out' – i.e. had been presented at court or, if not entitled to that honour, old enough to be at balls and so on – then the proper people to accompany her were either her mother, her father, her brother or some other suitable relation. Indeed, it was said more generally that most married ladies, particularly those who were young, often favoured walking with a companion as well.[4] This choice would not have been a matter of absolute propriety, but rather prudent discretion. A lady walking alone would naturally have drawn attention to herself. It would have been, as the etiquette thus far shows, an uncommon sight to passers-by. We could perhaps take from these pieces of etiquette guidance that any lady – if she was desirous to err on the side of caution when it came to her conduct whilst out and about – might have preferred to walk in the company of another respectable person.

Of course, the rules which applied in towns did not necessarily apply in the country. Whilst it would have been unthinkable for our aforementioned young lady to venture out alone in London, she could have gone between the houses of friends and relations on her own with complete respectability when she was in the country.[5] And whilst these particular points of etiquette have been addressed to ladies, gentlemen were not exempt from differing expectations of conduct between the town and country. It was one thing for a gentleman to whistle on a charming country lane, but such behaviour was simply not the done thing when he was in town.[6]

Thus far, we have covered how a lady or gentleman dressed for the street, the fashionable times for walking and that it was generally better for a lady to walk in the company of another person. These points of etiquette have generally concerned the behaviour expected in towns such as London and fashionable watering places. The next matter to which our attention shall turn is the etiquette of greeting and interacting with other ladies and gentlemen.

One particularly pressing matter of propriety was who a lady or gentleman was allowed to recognise in the street, and how they were allowed to recognise them. In many ways, this reflects the etiquette which surrounded introductions. Or at least, similarities in the logic of the etiquette can be seen. It also refers back to the importance of rank and precedence, which dominated the first chapter and which will continue to permeate through the rest of the book.

If two acquaintances came across one another on the street or whilst out walking, the person of superior rank had the right of recognition over the person of inferior rank. However, if the acquaintance existed between a lady and a gentleman, then the lady was always the one who had the right of recognition. This rule can be seen as an absolute maxim of propriety, and it was repeated throughout the century.

A gentleman had no business in greeting a lady, unless she had recognised him first. The only possible exception was where the acquaintance was very long-standing, intimate and familiar indeed. This point of etiquette should perhaps be viewed alongside the principle of introducing a gentleman to a lady and could be considered as an example of giving precedence to ladies as a matter of courtesy.

A lady would have indicated that she had seen a gentleman, and was acknowledging the acquaintance, with a slight bow or an inclination of her head. In return, a gentleman would then have bowed and lifted his hat entirely from his head. It was thought to be woefully insufficient conduct for a gentleman merely to touch the brim of his hat. If it was two gentlemen who were acknowledging each other in the street, then they would have nodded to one another.[7]

Let us suppose, for example, that a gentleman, Mr A, saw a friend of his coming towards him in one of the parks in London. This friend was a baronet, who we shall call Sir B. As the person of superior rank, Sir B took precedence in this situation and it was up to him to recognise his friend. Of course, Mr A was a lovely, affable fellow and Sir B was delighted to nod to him as he passed by. Mr A would then have nodded in return.

However, the situation would have been different if it had not been Mr A out walking, but rather his wife and daughter. Had Mrs A and Miss A been the ones approaching Sir B – presuming of course that they were also acquainted with him – then they would have been the ones to give the first token of recognition. Sir B, upon seeing them act, would have bowed and lifted his hat.

This delicate matter of greeting people in the streets was unfortunately linked to the sad and sorry business of 'cutting' them. This basically meant ending an acquaintance. For a lady or gentleman to cut an acquaintance was a serious matter indeed, and it was something probably best done after a period of careful reflection. It was not something which was supposed to be done rashly, in a moment of annoyance or anger.

There were nevertheless rules as to who people were allowed to cut from their circle of acquaintance. One basic rule was that a gentleman could never cut a lady. Additionally, a single lady could not cut a married one. *Mixing in Society* thought that cutting was something which was best avoided. If a lady or gentleman was plagued by a person saluting them in the street who they did not like, who they did not want to call upon, and who they thought was taking a gross impertinence in continually bowing to them, it was still better for the afflicted lady or gentleman to return the recognition. Rather than directly cutting the person, they were advised to return the salute in a cold and formal fashion. Doubtless, the offended lady or gentleman would have quietly hoped that the other person would eventually take the hint and leave them alone. This action was certainly less brutal than openly and publically cutting someone, which could go so far as to look a person in the eye and then turn away from them. That action essentially made it clear that someone had been acknowledged, and then dismissed.

However, there were many other aspects of etiquette pertaining to proper conduct whilst out and about. And, happily for us, they are generally far nicer to consider than the unpleasant business just discussed. One example was the recommendation that ladies and gentlemen should make a point of recognising and saluting people of lower rank.[8] For example, they were advised to take notice of people such as their dressmakers, tailors and those with whom they did business. It was a matter of politeness. Moreover, whilst a lady or gentleman might not have mixed in the same circles as a person in trade, or another profession or situation, that person was still perfectly respectable, decent and deserving of their civility and recognition.

Another matter of concern which ladies and gentlemen had to contend with in the nineteenth century is one which their twenty-first-century descendants in Great Britain still have to face. That is, of course, the question of how to deal with weather that seems generally disposed to be as grey, rainy and miserable as possible. Thus, as we have seen, ladies were advised to arm themselves with an umbrella in winter. Additionally, if they needed to manoeuvre their way through a particularly wet patch of the street, they were advised to lift the hem of their dress no higher than their ankle and to perform the delicate procedure with their right hand only.[9] We shall therefore presume that a lady concerned with the strictures of etiquette and modesty would never have abandoned them, even if it meant sacrificing the hem of her new dress to a puddle.

When streets were particularly wet and horrible, a lady or gentleman would have taken special care not to splash or otherwise inconvenience those around them. After all, it is not hard to imagine that it would have been rather trying for a lady, if she had just managed to navigate a puddle and save the hem on her new dress, to then have a foolish and careless lady splatter filth all over the new dress in the very next moment.

Gentlemen were also pressed to remember that umbrellas and canes were not toys to be swung about to the endangerment of all in the general vicinity. That the poor lady mentioned above, who had just had her dress ruined in one moment by one silly person, might then have been whacked about the shins by another is a situation so repugnant to anyone with a sense of etiquette (or, indeed, common decency) that the thought alone should illustrate the importance any lady or gentleman would have placed upon treating their fellow passers-by with the utmost consideration and respect.

Therefore, if a lady or gentleman needed to pass a person on the street, they would have done so on whichever side caused the other person the least inconvenience.[10] Whether a lady or gentleman passed a person on the left or right was irrelevant. It was the trouble they caused in doing so which mattered.

Ladies walking together would also have been considerate of other people using the street. Or at least, they should have been according to the guidance laid out in etiquette manuals. If three ladies went out together, two should have walked side by side and the remaining lady should have walked ever so slightly ahead of them.[11] It would have been very thoughtless of them to have walked along arm in arm and commandeered the whole width of the pavement.

Propriety also continued to be a consideration of paramount importance. However, if a lady was walking in the company of a gentleman, she could have accepted his arm in the knowledge that her conduct was perfectly correct.

It was felt that streets were not really suitable places to stop and talk. Stopping and making a cluster in the middle of the pavement had the potential to cause an obstacle in the path of people simply going about their business. And, as has already been discussed, inconveniencing other people was something to be avoided. Yet, if a lady or gentleman saw someone they knew and felt that they really did have to speak to them, then the best course of action would have been to walk with that person, even if it meant the lady or gentleman had to change the direction in which they had been walking. It would have been very wrong for a lady or gentleman to detain a friend or acquaintance who was trying to get somewhere, or to insist that their friend should change direction and walk in the opposite direction they needed to go, simply because the first lady or gentleman had suddenly remembered something they had to tell them.

With regard to talking to someone in the street, another principle of proper conduct was to be careful about saying the other person's name. Loudly proclaiming their name to whichever portion of the populace happened to be passing would have been exceedingly vulgar indeed. Ladies and gentlemen who felt the need to converse in the streets should have done so at a sensible, reasonable volume.

To illustrate this, we shall introduce Mr C and Mr D. If, after recognising one another, Mr C wished to converse with Mr D, then he would have fallen into step with Mr D and endeavoured not to delay him unnecessarily. So far, so good with regard to Mr C's adherence to the expectations of conduct set out in etiquette manuals. However, if Mr C had loudly spent the duration of the conversation using   Mr D's name as a punctuation mark at the end of each sentence, then we can imagine that Mr D would not have been best pleased by the end of it.

Of course, neither a lady nor a gentleman was limited to walking when out and about. Whilst they might have walked around a park for pleasure, or to simply get from A to B, a horse-drawn carriage was another mode of transport. And, like walking, carriage drives could be both a matter of leisure and necessity.

Indeed, driving a carriage was a popular pastime. Whilst a lady would most likely have contented herself with driving a carriage with one horse, some gentlemen enjoyed displaying their skill and dexterity by driving a team of four. Carriages were, after all, one of the must-have status symbols of the nineteenth century.

During the Season in London towards the end of the century, the fashionable hours to go driving were from 4.30 until 6.30, or even 7 o'clock.[12] In the winter, the preferred hours were between 2.30 and 5 o'clock, perhaps extending to 5.30. However, in the final years of the century, it was said more generally that the normal hours for driving were between 3 o'clock and 6.30 in the summer, and between 2.30 and 4.30 in the winter.[13]

It was felt that ladies who drove for pleasure tended to favour low phaetons or pony carriages, and that they should have been accompanied by a groom. He would then be able to hold the horse's head if the lady wanted to stop and talk to a friend, or to go into a shop. If a lady was driving about the streets of London, she would have done this in what was still considered to be the morning, between 12 o'clock and 2 o'clock.[14] It was said that once the roads became busy and crowded, it would have been impossible for her to enjoy the drive.

When ladies or gentlemen were out and about in a carriage there were some points of etiquette which they would have been obliged to take into account. Or at least, they would have been required to do so if they were adhering to the guidance put forward by etiquette manuals. Just as it was important to make sure that a lady was introduced to a gentleman, or that the superior in rank made the first greeting whilst out walking, it was also important for ladies and gentlemen to know their place – so to speak – when going to sit down in a carriage. We could perhaps see this as a further matter of rank and precedence.

A husband and wife driving in their own carriage would have sat facing the horses.[15] The seats facing the horses were considered to be the best seats. When a family was travelling together in a carriage, the mother and father would have sat facing the horses, and their children would have sat with their backs to the horses.[16] If a mother was travelling with her daughter, the daughter would only have sat next to her mother when there were no other ladies in the carriage with them.[17] If a daughter had been occupying the seat next to her mother and another lady joined them in the carriage, the daughter would have had to give up her seat and move to sit with her back facing the horses.[18] She would have done this even if her own rank was higher than that of the other lady. Also, if there were multiple daughters, then the eldest daughter would have taken precedence over her younger sisters and would have taken the seat facing the horses before them.[19]

If a lady or gentleman had guests in their carriage, then a hostess would have sat facing the horses.[20] However, a host would have given up his seat for any ladies and would have sat with his back to the horses.[21] Indeed, as a general rule in mixed company, ladies were given the best seats in the carriage. Gentlemen, being gentlemen, would have sacrificed their own comfort to the benefit of the ladies and would have sat with their backs to the horses. A gentleman would only have sat next to a lady, facing the horses, if there were no other ladies in the carriage with them.

Of course, there were exceptions. A very elderly gentleman could have been given a better seat, in preference to a lady who was also in the carriage.[22] Or, a hostess might have chosen to give her seat facing the horses to a gentleman, if she knew that sitting with his back to the horses was likely to make him feel unwell during the course of the journey.[23] A good hostess would always have been attentive to the needs of her guests.

In addition, there would have been times when there were more ladies than seats facing the horses. In circumstances such as those, it seems that seats would generally have been distributed according to precedence. A hostess would have sat facing the horses. If she had two other ladies travelling with her, then the lady of highest distinction would have sat next to the hostess and the other lady would have sat with her back to the horses. So, if one lady was married and the other unmarried, then the married lady would have sat next to the hostess.

There were also some points of etiquette regarding entering and leaving a carriage. When a hostess had guests, she would have allowed them to enter the carriage first.[24] When leaving a carriage, gentlemen would have got out first, so that they could assist any ladies in stepping down.

Whilst not strictly a matter of etiquette, long-distance travel by carriage was part of nineteenth-century life for ladies and gentlemen. This was not only true at the beginning of the century, but remained the case even after the introduction of the railway. The railway did not cover the country overnight, and therefore there would have been plenty of instances in which it was not a viable option for a journey.

ELEGANT ETIQUETTE IN THE NINETEENTH CENTURY

A long carriage journey could have been undertaken in a number of forms. If a lady or gentleman was possessed of the luxury of their own carriage, they would have been able to arrange their own transport. However, this could be a slow option as a lady's or gentleman's horses would have needed to stop and rest. Another option was to travel by post-chaise. The chaise would have stopped at regular intervals, so that the horses could be changed and the travellers could continue on their journey without delay. This was a faster option, but also a costly one. For those who did not have sufficient means to travel in their own carriage or by post-chaise, travelling on the stagecoach was an alternative option. Travel by stagecoach was cheaper, but it was also slower.

Railways became increasingly popular and more accessible over the course of the century. Yet they posed a threat to the accepted standards of etiquette, which decried overfamiliarity in the strongest possible terms. Ladies and gentlemen travelling on a train might have found that strangers actually tried to talk to them. Ladies and gentlemen were advised to tolerate this as long as the other person was clearly a respectable individual. However, a conversation on a train was not an introduction, and it did not mean the beginning of an acquaintance. Any interaction between two people, which began on a train, ended once they had left the train.

Some Principal Points of Politeness
- Ladies were advised to be restrained in their style of dress.
- If two acquaintances saw each other whilst out and about, it was the person of superior rank who was supposed to acknowledge the acquaintance first.
- However, if those two people were a lady and a gentleman, then it fell to the lady to recognise the acquaintance. In that instance, their respective ranks became irrelevant.
- In greeting a lady, a gentleman was supposed to bow and lift his hat entirely from his head.
- Ladies and gentlemen were supposed to be considerate of their fellow passers-by.

CHAPTER THREE

- If a lady or gentleman wanted to talk to someone, they were supposed to walk with them, even if that meant the first lady or gentleman had to change direction. They were not supposed to detain the other person.
- In a carriage, ladies would have been given better seats in preference to gentlemen.
- Gentlemen would have got out of the carriage first, to help ladies down.
- Any interaction between two people on a train ended with the conclusion of the journey.

CHAPTER FOUR

The Important Business of Paying Calls and Leaving Cards

The practice of paying calls and leaving cards was a significant aspect of ladies' and gentlemen's social lives in the nineteenth century. It made up part of the fabric of their social world. It would have been something familiar to them, part of the accepted pattern of normal life. If looking at etiquette is a way to explore and attempt to understand what life was like for ladies and gentlemen during the nineteenth century, then considering this central social convention will be instrumental to that endeavour. As we shall see in the course of this chapter, paying calls and leaving cards was in many ways a cyclical process. This is because both were usually meant to be reciprocated. Thus, the paying of calls and the leaving of cards can be viewed as a ritual which kept social interaction turning, rather like a wheel. Consequently, as well as being a familiar ritual, it would also have been an important one. Or at least, ladies and gentlemen who were concerned with following the rules of etiquette, and who wanted to socialise, would most likely have placed importance on the practice.

However, before the wider etiquette can be properly explored, some of the principles – perhaps we might say the form, substance and even the terminology – of paying calls and leaving cards must be discussed. This means considering matters such as what a call was, what a card looked like and what it meant to be 'not at home'. In terms of trying to imagine the nineteenth-century world and nineteenth-century life, this consideration of physical objects as well as customs and habits will hopefully lend further depth to the picture we are painting.

As mentioned above, the first matter to contend with must be a discussion of what a call actually was and why one might have been paid. At a very basic level, to call upon another person simply meant to go to their house and visit them. The reason for doing this was that paying and returning calls formed an exchange of polite attentions and civilities. We have already discussed the etiquette of introductions, and whilst an introduction could not really be un-made, the resulting acquaintance might have come to very little if a lady or gentleman did not attempt to maintain and improve it. Of course, if a lady or gentleman wanted to have nothing to do with the rest of the world, then that was their business. But, we can reasonably presume that most people would have wanted to have something in the way of a circle of friends and acquaintances.

Whilst calls were fundamentally paid to maintain an acquaintance and might have been paid as a matter of course, there would have been times when they were paid for a particular reason. For instance, one acquaintance might have called upon another to offer congratulations for a happy event, or to offer condolences if there had been a bereavement. This follows a similar logic to what is generally considered polite now. If a couple announces their engagement on social media and it gets no response from their friends, they are likely to feel somewhat slighted. On a more general level, if we send a friend an email or text to catch-up and they never reply, most of us would probably feel disappointed.

The next topic for consideration is what a card actually was, what it would have looked like and what it would have been used for. Simply put, cards explained who a person was and were left to inform an acquaintance that the person named on the card had been to their house. Or, as might have been the case when a gentleman's card was left, that his wife had been to their house. But we shall say more about that later. It is the form and style of cards which interests us at this juncture.

In the second half of the century, ladies and gentlemen were told to keep their cards plain and simple. Shiny, glazed cards were declared to be completely out of fashion and most distasteful. Extravagant writing, coronets, crests and monograms were not supposed to be added to cards either.

The next important detail for the form of a calling card was the bearer's name and title. In the 1870s, *Mixing in Society* suggested that some gentlemen were dropping the 'Mr' from their cards and that some unmarried ladies were omitting the 'Miss', and advised that these were good practices to adopt. However, there were etiquette manuals in both the 1880s and 1890s which instructed ladies and gentlemen to have both their name and title printed on their card. This included the titles of 'Mr', 'Mrs' and 'Miss'.

Baronets, knights and other individuals who held titles of rank would also have included these titles on their cards. The only exception was the courtesy title 'the Honourable', which was not supposed to be used in this instance. Honorary titles, such as the letters MP for a Member of Parliament, would not have appeared on cards either. However, gentlemen who held professional titles and military or naval ranks would have put these on their cards.

According to advice given in the final two decades of the century, a first name would normally have been added if there was a need for a lady or gentleman to distinguish their card from that of another relation. So, if a gentleman needed to make sure that his card was not mistaken for his father's, he would have added his first name. His card would therefore have read 'Mr William Baker', for example. If his wife needed to ensure that her card was not taken to be her mother-in-law's card then her card would have read 'Mrs William Baker'. A wife would have used her husband's first name, not her own.

There were some instances in which people might have shared cards. Therefore, multiple names would have been printed on them. So, for example, it was considered inappropriate for a young and unmarried lady to have her own cards. Instead, her name would have been added to her mother's card. So, if there was one daughter in a family, her mother's card might have read 'Mrs Smith and Miss Smith'.[1] If there was more than one daughter, the card might have had 'Mrs Smith and The Misses Smith' printed on it.[2] Alternatively, the card could have said 'Mrs Smith, Miss Smith and Miss Elizabeth Smith'.[3] The latter example once again demonstrates the custom of distinguishing the eldest daughter from her younger sisters.

Some married couples also shared cards when they paid calls together. However, *Etiquette: What to Do and How to Do It* considered this to be a waning practice by the 1880s. It was said that this custom was only really seen in places such as country towns, and that even then the couple would often have had individual cards for when they paid calls separately.

The next important piece of information contained on cards was the bearer's address. The guidance given towards the end of the period was that a person's name was printed in the centre of the card. Their address was then printed in the left-hand corner. If they had a second address, this was then printed in the right-hand corner. These conventions applied to both ladies and gentlemen.

Yet, gentlemen did have some additional factors to bear in mind. If a gentleman was a member of a club, he could – if he so desired – have put the name thereof in the right-hand corner.[4] His address would then have appeared, as normal, in the left-hand corner. Alternative guidance from the very final years of the century suggested that the name of a gentleman's club could simply be printed below his address, in the left-hand corner.[5]

If a gentleman was an officer of a regiment and wished this to be known on his card, then following the guidelines for clubs he would have put the regiment on the right and his address on the left.[6] If a gentleman belonged to both a regiment and a club, and was desirous to have all of these details included on his card, then he was advised to put the regiment on the right, his address on the left, and his club on the left underneath his address.[7] Naturally, ladies were exempt from having to consider making additions such as these to their cards.

The final matters with which we have to contend here are the terms 'at home' and 'not at home', because they had very little to do with whether or not a lady or gentleman was actually in their house. Although it is perfectly plausible that a lady or gentleman might have called upon another person, only to be told by a servant that the master or mistress was 'not at home' because they really had gone out, the phrase was generally used to politely convey that someone was not available to receive visitors. When they were told that a person was 'not at home', a lady or gentleman would have understood that this was not an insult or a slight.

Early on in this period, Trusler claimed in *A System of Etiquette* that some people chose only to be 'at home' to those with whom they were already on very intimate terms. Later on in the century, *Mixing in Society* said that it was best practice to try and receive all visitors who paid a call. However, there was also the custom of having set days when a lady was 'at home' to receive company. This custom did have the benefit of enabling friends and acquaintances to pay calls upon ladies knowing that they would be able to receive them, and thus saved people from disappointment and wasted journeys.

The distinction between 'at home' and 'not at home' was not just for the benefit of the person standing on the doorstep, to tell them whether or not they could go into the house. Whether or not the person asked if the master or mistress was 'at home' determined if they were paying a call, and thus hoping to go in, or if they were only leaving a card for them. Sometimes, people would simply call to leave a card for another person, with no intention of going into their house. In this case, the person leaving a card would have handed it to the servant saying, 'For Lady Brown', or the name of whoever was the intended recipient. Leaving cards was a polite attention and social nicety. If a lady or gentleman did not ask to go into a house, it did not (automatically) mean that they were implying something negative about the acquaintance.

However, this analysis of what really must be seen as the procedural background to paying calls and leaving cards is only the beginning. The bracketed 'automatically' in the paragraph above is perhaps indicative of this. The etiquette of paying calls and leaving cards was extensive, and differing habits and practices can be seen through the century. Yet, now that we have considered the fundamental principles of this piece of nineteenth-century social life – what it meant to be 'at home' and 'not at home', what a card might have looked like, that sometimes people might have called for friendship, that sometimes people might have had to pay a call as a matter of social obligation, and that sometimes people might have simply left cards as a business separate to paying calls – we have a starting point from which we can branch out into the deeper intricacies of etiquette concerning these matters.

This exploration must begin with the delicate matter of who was allowed to call upon whom. Of foremost importance was that a lady would have never paid a call upon a gentleman. The only possible exception to this rule would have been a situation in which a lady was obliged to call upon a gentleman owing to either a professional or official matter. It does not require a great leap of conjecture, at this point, to suppose that ladies and gentlemen might have been pleased that some rules of etiquette were quite clear and simple to follow.

Another rule relates once more to the issue of precedence. Between two individuals, it was the superior in rank who would have left the first card at the address of the person of lower rank. When it came to extending the acquaintance, it was the privilege of the person of higher rank to propose that a call could be made.

If a lady paid a call upon a lady superior to her in rank, who had only left a card at her address, this would have been a decided impropriety and breach of etiquette. In contrast, if the aforementioned lady of lower rank left a card at the address of the lady of higher rank – we are of course assuming that she was leaving a card in return for having received one herself – and the lady of higher rank then paid her a call, this would have been a real compliment from the higher ranking lady.

Let us say, for example, that Mrs A was introduced to Lady B by a mutual friend. We shall imagine that Mrs A is a commoner and that Lady B is the wife of a baronet. Lady B then left a card at Mrs A's address. Mrs A, perhaps thinking she had left a rather more favourable impression upon Lady B than was actually the case, determined that she would pay a call upon Lady B. According to our understanding of etiquette, Mrs A would have been acting in serious error, and Lady B could have quite possibly concluded that Mrs A had behaved in an overly familiar or impertinent manner. It would have also looked rather presuming if Mrs A had decided to leave a card before Lady B had left one first.

However, let us return to the initial example. If upon receiving her card, Mrs A had simply left a return card, and it was Lady B who took the initiative to pay a call upon Mrs A, then the situation would have been quite the reverse. Mrs A could rightly have thought herself rather flattered.

Another instance where etiquette dictated who could call upon whom and – of equal importance – who could not call upon whom, was when someone new took up residence in a neighbourhood. The rule which seems to have echoed down the century was that newcomers needed to wait for the established residents of a locality to pay the first call upon them, or to leave the first card. This rule held true, even if the newcomer was of a higher social rank. According to advice dating to the later years of the century, paying a call upon a newcomer suggested that one wanted to be on friendly terms, whilst leaving a card implied one wished the acquaintance to be of a more ceremonial nature.

Once the newcomer had received the compliment of a call or card, the polite thing to do was to reciprocate the civility as soon as possible. If the newcomer to the area had received a call and was not desirous to pursue the acquaintance, then they could have left a card in return for the call. This was a polite response, but showed that they did not want to be on more intimate terms. Equally, the established resident could do the same thing in reverse, or simply not call again.

Thus, if a Mr C were to have purchased an estate, he would have waited for the surrounding gentlemen to call upon him. He would not have simply turned up at another resident's house, to tell them that he was their new neighbour. This was, at least, the rule which applied in the country and in country towns. In towns and cities such as London, it was expected that a lady or gentleman would let their circle of acquaintance know of their arrival by calling or leaving cards.

A further component of the etiquette of calling and of leaving cards was the significance of responding to them in a timely fashion. It is important to stress that if a person had received a call or card, they were supposed to respond. To ignore the civility extended in either of these forms would have been really quite discourteous. In the later years of the nineteenth century, it was suggested that a call needed to be returned with a call and that a card needed to be returned with a card. Ideally, this would have been done within a week. We can therefore see a pattern of calls being paid and cards being left in a circular and reciprocal fashion, as mentioned at the start of this chapter.

In addition to this, and according to etiquette advice from the later decades of the century, if a lady returned a call with only a card then she was intimating that the acquaintance should not grow closer and should be of a slight nature.[8] However, it was suggested in the 1870s that a ceremonial call – which can be explained as a call paid out of civility as opposed to a call paid out of particular friendship – could be returned by a card, as long as the lady or gentleman doing so made a point of asking after the health of the family when the servant answered the door.[9] In the 1830s *Etiquette for Gentlemen* was still more relaxed on this matter, and advised that a gentleman could return a visit with a card with perfect propriety. This clearly underlines that etiquette was not uniform or fixed throughout the century. What was considered polite could change. By extension, it would have been perfectly possible for people, perhaps of different generations, to hold different views on what was polite or appropriate. Nevertheless, all of these examples indicate that some sort of response was needed throughout the century, in order not to be in breach of etiquette.

The importance of responding, and of doing so in a timely fashion, is additionally demonstrated in the exactitude with which ladies were advised to record calls paid and cards left in the second half of the century. Preferably, they would have kept a precise account of when they paid calls or left cards, and would in turn have recorded when they received a response. In this way, ladies would have been able to keep track of how their calls and cards were received, and could judge if they were visiting or leaving cards too little or too often. Of course, it was important to take into account cases where the other party might be infirm or unwell. In this instance, it was important for a lady to keep up the regularity of her visits. It should be said that the practice of leaving cards was considered to be a largely, although of course not exclusively, female occupation. Gentlemen's attention was presumably taken up by affairs of business, or other lofty concerns. It was really only bachelors who had to shift for themselves in these matters.

The importance of tracking calls and cards can also be seen in the advice given in relation to servants. At the beginning of the century, Trusler explained in *A System of Etiquette* that the custom of leaving cards when people were 'not at home' developed as a way of showing that a lady or gentleman had been to a house. Cards meant that there was something to show for the visit and could prevent a servant from forgetting to tell their employer of the call, or aid them in instances where there had been too many calls for the servant to reasonably be expected to remember all of them. In short, cards were a way of stopping people from being disappointed or feeling slighted.

By the later decades of the century, *Etiquette: What to Do and How to Do It* advised that servants should be instructed to keep a tally of who had paid a call and asked if the master or mistress was 'at home', and who had called to leave cards. Again, it was pointed out that some houses could receive more calls and cards in one afternoon than a servant could feasibly recall.

However, as well as responding to all calls paid to them and all cards left for them, there were times when a lady or gentleman would have been particularly expected to extend these civilities to their friends and acquaintances. For instance, it was important to pay calls to offer congratulations for a happy event, such as news of an engagement within a family. On such an occasion, a lady or gentleman was supposed to pay a call and give their warm congratulations.

A further example of this, which has been mentioned previously, was the importance of expressing condolences after a bereavement. Generally, it was thought best for a lady or gentleman to leave a card with the bereaved family in the first instance, unless they were also a family member or a very close friend. This attention was supposed to be paid within a week of the loss taking place, or ideally as soon after the loss has taken place as possible. A personal visit would have been paid after receiving a card of thanks from the family, which indicated that they were once again ready to receive visitors. It was also suggested that calls to offer condolences could be paid after the family had been seen to attend public worship, if a lady or gentleman had only a slight acquaintance with them.

Furthermore, some etiquette manuals suggested that there were certain times of the year when calls should have been paid or cards should have been left. In the middle of the century, *Etiquette, Social Ethics and the Courtesies of Society* felt the traditional custom of paying calls at Christmas and New Year was one which ought to be maintained. In the 1880s, *Etiquette: What to Do and How to Do It* said that in London cards were supposed to be left before Easter and then again after Easter, which coincided with the start of the Season.

In addition, ladies and gentlemen were expected to let their acquaintance know that they had arrived in town – for example, in London for the Season – by calling or by leaving cards. They were also supposed to inform their acquaintance of their departure from a place in a similar manner. Advice given towards the beginning of the century said that cards left in those circumstances should have 'to take leave' written on them.[10] Etiquette manuals from the second half of the century felt that the abbreviation 'P.P.C.' ought to have been used. 'P.P.C.' stood for '*pour prendre congé*', which translates from the French as 'to take leave'.

Of course, it was all well and good for a lady or gentleman to know when to pay a call or leave a card, but there were further points of good conduct that they were advised to take into account. Behaving with perfect propriety and civility required no small amount of effort.

The first matter which faced a lady or gentleman was the question of when to pay a call. This does not mean remembering to mark certain occasions, as we have just discussed, but rather paying a call at the right time of day. Whilst the system of paying calls in the nineteenth century is often referred to as 'morning calls', this title is something of a misnomer. To a modern individual, at least, the hours suggested are not morning hours at all.

One piece of advice from the first half of the century was that, when paying a call to a lady, the call should be made between the hours of 2 o'clock and 4 o'clock.[11] However, within the same time period, it was suggested that the fashionable time to pay calls was between 1 o'clock and 4 o'clock.[12] However, later on in the century, the time period for paying calls seems to have become later. One manual from the 1870s told its readers that calls should be paid between 3 o'clock and 5 o'clock.[13] Also in the 1870s, a further manual made a distinction between the seasons. According to that advice, calls paid in winter should take place between 2 o'clock and 4 o'clock.[14] In the summer, this was extended and calls were supposed to be made between 2 o'clock to 5 o'clock. In the 1880s, another manual distinguished between three types of call. Their advice was that calls could be ceremonious calls to slight acquaintances, semi-ceremonious calls to acquaintances of longer duration, and unceremonious calls to intimate friends.[15] Across these three groups, the correct time periods for paying calls were between 3 o'clock and 4 o'clock, between 3 o'clock and 5 o'clock, and from 4 o'clock to either 6 o'clock or 6.30 respectively. In the final decade of this era, *The Manners and Rules of Good Society* suggested that calls should be paid between 3 o'clock and 6 o'clock, whilst alternative advice suggested that the correct timeframe for paying calls was between 4 o'clock and 7 o'clock.[16] To be a little tongue-in-cheek, a good course of action during the nineteenth century might have been for ladies and gentlemen to have played it safe by only calling upon people at precisely 4 o'clock.

Certain behaviours were also expected – or were at least advised – in the process of paying a call or leaving a card. We have already addressed the matter of being 'at home' or 'not at home' on a basic level. However, there were some additional formalities surrounding the practice of finding out if someone was indeed 'at home' or 'not at home', and then either paying a call or leaving cards.

To begin, if a lady was only intending to leave cards, neither she nor her servant would have asked if the person in question was 'at home'. Instead, they or their servant would have simply handed over the cards saying, as an example, 'For Mrs D'.

However, let us suppose that a hypothetical lady decided that she wished to call upon her friend. When the servant answered the door, she would have asked if her friend was 'at home'. If she had gone out in her carriage, she would have sent her servant to the door to make the enquiry on her behalf.

If the servant answering the door responded in the negative, cards would then have been left. However, a lady or gentleman could have left more than one card. In the first half of the century, *Etiquette for Gentlemen* explained that whilst the normal habit was to leave one card, more would be left if there was a guest staying, or if a gentleman particularly wished to indicate that the visit was intended for both the master and mistress when he was only acquainted with one of them. Generally speaking, a popular practice seems to have been leaving one card for each person to whom the compliment of the visit was intended, i.e. one card for the master, one card for the mistress and then further cards as applicable for anyone else residing within the house. For example, a lady or gentleman might have left a card for a grown-up daughter of the house, or for a guest who happened to be staying there. Advice from the final decades of the century suggested that if the person was 'not at home', then the lady paying the call would have left three cards.[17] She would have left one of her own cards and two of her husband's. Presumably, her card would have been for the mistress of the establishment, while her husband's cards would have been for the mistress and the master.

Interestingly, the custom of turning down cards was declared obsolete a number of times throughout the century. In the second half on the 1830s, *Hints on Etiquette* suggested that whilst some people still turned down the corner of a card to show that they had intended to call upon more than one person, leaving multiple cards was preferable to this. Yet, at around the same time, *Etiquette for Gentlemen* declared the practice to be completely out of fashion. *Etiquette for Gentlemen* also explained the custom of turning down cards slightly differently. According to their version of the practice, turning down one corner indicated that the visit was to only one person in the house – for instance, to either the husband or the wife – whilst folding down two corners or one side of the card showed that the visit had been meant for both. In *All About Etiquette* from the 1870s, readers were instructed not to turn down corners because it was an outmoded practice. Yet, in the 1880s and again in the 1890s, guidance regarding the etiquette of turning down corners was given once more. Here, turning down the right-hand corner was said to indicate that the call was for all the ladies of the house and not just the mistress.[18] *Etiquette: What to Do and How to Do It* also said that turning down a corner demonstrated that the call had been made personally, and not by a servant.

Whilst turning down corners may have been a part of the etiquette of leaving cards known to, or practised by, ladies and gentlemen throughout the century, it does not seem unreasonable to suggest that it was a varied and changing custom. Perhaps turning down corners was one of those unfortunate matters where, sometimes, a person could not do right for doing wrong.

However, let us take a few steps back in time and return to the hypothetical lady who was trying to pay a call on her friend. Instead of discovering that her friend was 'not at home', let us imagine that she was indeed receiving visitors. Upon hearing this piece of welcome information from her friend's servant, the lady would have then entered into the house.

Once inside, the next point of etiquette to which a lady or gentleman would have had to attend was what to do with hats and bonnets and other items of outerwear. As a general rule, a lady would not have removed any part of her attire for the duration of her call, even when asked to do so by the mistress of the house after she had been received. The most she would have been allowed to remove would have been a scarf around her neck or a boa. Shawls and bonnets absolutely had to stay in place. The only exception was when she was visiting a particular friend, and then only if her friend asked her to do so.

Gentlemen were advised to take their hat with them into the room, because leaving it in the hallway would look like they were making themselves too much at home. Once he had been received, a gentleman could have either kept hold of his hat in one hand, or he could have placed it on the floor. According to *Mixing in Society* in the 1870s, he would have been very wrong to put it on a chair, table, pianoforte or any other piece of furniture. However, later advice suggested that this behaviour was acceptable.[19] Gentlemen were also advised to keep canes and sticks with them. However, overcoats could be left in the hallway.[20]

In order to be presented to the master or mistress, a lady or gentleman would have followed the servant and had their arrival announced to the relevant person. According to *Manners and Rules of Good Society* in the 1890s, a gentleman paying a call would have been announced as 'Mr E'. His wife would have been 'Mrs E'. If Mr E had been a baronet or a knight, he would have been announced as 'Sir E'. This announcement would have included both his first name and his surname. His wife would have been announced as 'Lady E', although this would only have included her surname. Peers would have been introduced as 'Lord F', rather than as 'the Earl of F' or 'Viscount F'. A peeress would have been announced in the corresponding fashion. Indeed, the only title which was not used was the courtesy title 'the Honourable'.

Once received, the business at hand was largely that of making polite conversation and generally being agreeable. Of course, however well the conversation was going, a lady or gentleman would have needed to be careful about staying too long. The duration of a call was a significant point of etiquette. Whilst it might have looked bad to stay for too little time, it was also necessary not to outstay one's welcome. Ladies and gentlemen were advised to pick up on important social cues, which suggested when it might be a good time to leave. Sensing that the conversation was beginning to flag, for example, might have indicated that it was time to get going. Alternatively, the arrival of other guests could have been a prompt for a lady or gentleman to begin to think about taking their leave.

Indeed, the ideal duration of a call could be seen as something of a hot topic in nineteenth-century etiquette. Right at the beginning of the century in *A System of Etiquette*, Trusler announced that the proper duration of a ceremonial call was between 15 and 20 minutes. Visits between close friends would naturally have followed their own course. This advice was echoed in the 1830s and 1840s.[21] Although in 1838, *Etiquette for Gentlemen* simply encouraged its readers to keep their visits brief. In the 1850s, it was suggested that visits of ceremony could be successfully completed within 30 minutes.[22] However, in the 1860s, *Etiquette for All* said that they should last no longer than 15 minutes. Alternative advice in the 1860s suggested that 15 to 20 minutes was an acceptable length of time to allot to a call.[23] In the 1870s, half an hour was once again advised.[24] In the 1890s, it was suggested that ceremonial calls should last for 15 minutes.[25] During the same decade, it was more generally advised that calls were not supposed to last for more than half an hour.[26]

It is clear that suggestions for how long a call should last were not identical throughout the century. That is only natural. Yet it seems fair to conclude that ladies and gentlemen were advised to be aware of how long they were lingering in other people's houses, and to avoid taking up too much of their time. And, broadly speaking, a call seems to have had a maximum time limit of 30 minutes. However, we can easily imagine this would have been waived if two very good friends wanted to have a very good chat.

Nevertheless, as well as their instructions on how to get things right, we must also consider what etiquette manuals said with regard to getting things wrong. Suffice to say, it was recommended that ladies and gentlemen tried to avoid committing certain unfortunate blunders.

The grim weather which seems on occasion determined to prevail year-round in Great Britain has indeed been mentioned before. And now it must be mentioned again. *Mixing in Society* felt that ladies and gentlemen should have refrained from paying calls in poor weather, unless they were so fortunate as to possess a closed carriage. It was thought that turning up at someone's house, drenched to the bone, dripping water over their floors and trailing mud in one's wake, was a breach of good manners which was best avoided.

In addition, it was said that children and dogs were best left at home. Both dogs and children were thought to be unsuitable participants in morning calls, and both were thought to have too great a potential to leave destruction in their wake. Even if they did not wreak havoc, the hostess would most likely spend the call worrying that they would. In short, taking dogs and children on calls was basically a bad idea all round.

CHAPTER FOUR

Thus far, we have considered what constituted good behaviour for ladies and gentlemen who were paying calls. However, we must also bear in mind the conduct which was expected of ladies and gentlemen when they received calls.

Ladies were advised to make sure they were ready to receive guests, if they intended to be 'at home'. Therefore, if ladies wore clothes that were quite clearly intended for work in the morning – i.e. for superintending servants and overseeing their tasks – then they should have made sure they had changed into clothing which was suitable for receiving company by the time they could start to expect calls to be made.

Aside from being appropriately attired, it was also important to receive guests in the proper manner. According to advice given in the 1860s, if the caller shown into the room was a gentleman, then the master of the house, or any other gentlemen present, should have stood to welcome him. If the caller was a lady, then both the master and mistress, and any other ladies and gentlemen in attendance, should have stood to receive her.

Hosts also needed to pay attention to their guests. Therefore, unless the visitor was a particularly close friend, ladies were advised to lay aside any needlework or other occupations for the duration of the call. It is not hard to see how people might have thought their call was unappreciated, or even unnoticed, if the hostess spent the call puzzling her way through a particularly complex section of her embroidery. However, it was possible to take a more relaxed point of view. Thus, assuming that a lady's needlework would not have consumed her attention, some believed that it was an acceptable activity to continue. It would not have been acceptable to continue activities such as drawing, painting or playing an instrument, as these activities were thought to be so naturally engrossing as to preclude the possibility of continuing them whilst at the same time paying a sufficient degree of attention to guests.

That it was best not to start introducing callers to one another has already been discussed in a previous chapter. However, if it did so happen that unacquainted people were present at the same time, then the host or hostess could not have simply buried their heads in the sand and pretended that the awkward situation was not happening. It thus seems prudent to revisit the etiquette of such an occurrence. In those circumstances, one way of handling the situation would have been to address each caller, or party of callers, in turn. That way, no one looked or felt neglected, and no one had a new acquaintance foisted upon them without their consent. *The Ladies Pocket Book of Etiquette* stressed during the first half of the century that it was important to treat guests equally, and that if any distinction was made, it should be made in favour of the greatest stranger.

Having successfully entertained their callers, a lady or gentleman would then have had to make sure they showed them the appropriate degree of civility as they left the house. It was a breach of etiquette to expect someone, to put it bluntly, to simply see themselves out. A more fitting course of action was for the host or hostess to ring for a servant to show any guests out.

Some Principal Points of Politeness

- Paying calls and leaving cards were civilities which were regularly and reciprocally exchanged.
- A lot of the time, this social civility was carried out by ladies.
- Ideally, a card would have been plain and simple.
- Generally, it was best to return a call with a call and a card with a card.
- A call or a card also needed to be returned in a timely fashion. So, for example, within a week.
- Ladies were advised to keep a clear record of calls and cards.
- If a lady or gentleman was 'not at home', this was not an insult. It did not mean that the lady or gentleman did not want to see that particular caller, but that they were not disposed to receive callers at that time.
- A call was not normally supposed to last longer than half an hour.
- If paying a call, a gentleman would not have left his hat in the hallway.
- Callers were advised to leave their dogs and children at home.

CHAPTER FIVE

The Art of Dining with Delicacy

The etiquette of the dining table had the potential to be a rather delicate matter. In the 1830s, *Hints on Etiquette* pointed out that what was considered to be in good taste at one moment was then declared woefully out of fashion in the next. And, on top of that, some people had a rather troublesome habit of being absolutely sure that their way of doing things at the dining table was the right way, regardless of what anyone else thought. In short, this does seem to suggest that the rules of etiquette were not set in stone. However, this chapter will nevertheless explore the etiquette advice, as it was laid down in contemporary guides, and will endeavour to offer up an outline of what it might have been like to dine as a lady or gentleman in the nineteenth century. Interestingly, some of the etiquette which will be considered here may well be familiar to the modern reader.

The first point of etiquette to consider is that of inviting guests. When throwing a dinner party, ladies and gentlemen would have been wise to be circumspect when choosing their guests. To be blunt, they were advised to select guests they thought were likely to get along. Unless a lady or gentleman was desirous of having their dinner remembered for all the wrong reasons, this was probably not the time or place to risk uniting bitter rivals, feuding siblings or jilted lovers.

Once the guests had been chosen, a further business to undertake was the issuing of invitations. At the beginning of the century, *A System of Etiquette* suggested that the correct wording for such invitations was to request the honour of a superior's company, the honour or favour of an equal's company and the compliment of an inferior's company. Later on, *Etiquette: What to Do and How to Do It* advised that invitations could request the pleasure of another person's company. Where applicable, invitations needed to be addressed to both the master and mistress of an establishment.

Invitations also needed to be sent out in a timely fashion. The size and scale of the dinner was an important factor to take into consideration. A large and formal dinner, perhaps given at the height of the Season in London, would have required a longer period of notice than a smaller and more informal gathering. Yet, varying guidance as to the appropriate amount of notice was issued throughout the century. Ten days to a fortnight was suggested, as a general rule.[1] However, two or three days was also put forward as an option.[2] A week to ten days notice was suggested for an informal dinner, whilst two or preferably three weeks' notice was recommended for a formal dinner.[3] In the final decade of the century, it was suggested that dinner invitations were being sent out up to six weeks in advance during the Season or when a large dinner was planned.[4]

However, there was at least one point about invitations that was definitely clear. If a lady or gentleman received an invitation to dinner, they needed to reply to it as soon as possible. Indeed, *Etiquette: What to Do and How to Do It* instructed its readers to not let a single post pass, without sending their response with it. After all, by delaying their answer, a lady or gentleman was leaving some poor, unfortunate hostess to try and organise a dinner – to try and arrange the food, the seating arrangements and the order of precedence – without even being sure of how many of her possible guests would actually be able to attend. It is therefore not hard to imagine why neglecting to respond might have come across as thoughtless and rude. When replying to an invitation to dinner, ladies and gentlemen were instructed to address their answer to the mistress of the house.

The next point of etiquette to which we shall turn our attention is the conduct which was expected of ladies and gentlemen when arriving at a dinner party and when going into the dining room. After all, a lady or gentleman would not have simply marched through the door, past the host and hostess, sat down at the table and commenced eating. Indeed, such conduct would have come across as peculiar, to say the least.

CHAPTER FIVE

To begin, just as it was important to respond to invitations in a timely fashion, it was also important to arrive on time for a dinner. At the beginning of the century, guests were advised that they should endeavour to arrive 15 minutes before the allotted hour for dinner.[5] The advice went so far as to exhort gentlemen to double-check that their pocket watch was running on time. Equally, it was important not to arrive too early. In the late 1830s, *Etiquette for Gentlemen* stressed that a gentleman who arrived too soon risked imposing himself upon an unsuspecting hostess when she might not be ready to receive guests. It was even suggested that if a gentleman arrived and realised that he was too early, then he should pretend he had mislaid the invitation and was simply calling to enquire as to the hour of dinner, so that he would not be late. Towards the end of the century, it was suggested that arriving 15 minutes beyond the hour appointed on the invitation was the latest acceptable time at which a guest might make their appearance.[6] And, although a lady might have been excused if she was half an hour late, a gentleman would have received no such leniency.[7]

It was thought rude and snobbish to keep others waiting, especially when such an action seemed to be derived from a desire on the part of the tardy lady or gentleman to appear superior to the rest of the company attending the dinner party. To illustrate this, let us imagine that in some unremarkable country town an unremarkable gentleman of business had lived peaceably and politely with his neighbours for many years. For whatever reason, he found himself honoured with a knighthood. Having previously been diligently punctual when invited to dine by those of his acquaintance, he suddenly began to arrive late and seemed to take some sort of pride in seeing his friends awaiting his arrival. Well, what could his circle of acquaintance have thought about this change in his behaviour? If they wanted to make the best of it, they might have thought him ridiculous. Equally, they might have thought it showed an unpleasant streak of self-importance and ill-breeding which had hitherto escaped their notice.

After arriving, ladies and gentlemen would have been presented in the room where the guests were assembling. This would normally have been the drawing room. According to advice given in the later stages of the century, if a party of guests arrived – perhaps a family with grown-up children or a husband and wife – then it was important that any ladies entered the room ahead of any gentlemen. It was indicative of poor taste if a lady and gentleman entered side by side. As guests entered the room, they would have been announced by the butler, or some other suitable servant, if the host and hostess did not keep a large establishment. However, although gentlemen followed ladies, they were still announced first. Thus, if we take the example of husband and wife, they would have been announced as 'Mr and Mrs A'. If Mr and Mrs A were attending with their daughter, then they would have been announced as 'Mr and Mrs and Miss A'.

The hostess would have welcomed the lady first and the gentleman second. Arriving guests were also told to greet the mistress of the house first, before anyone else. After all, it is not difficult to comprehend that a hostess might have felt slighted if guests, after being announced in her drawing room, then proceeded to ignore her.

Once all the diners were assembled in the drawing room, the next matter of etiquette which needs to be explored is how those diners would have made their way to the dining room. This is yet another instance in which etiquette returns, once more, to the subject of rank and precedence.

As a general rule, ladies and gentlemen would have gone into the dining room according to their order of precedence. Or at least, the highest ranking individuals would have been distinguished in some way. However, different etiquette manuals put forward different advice over the course of the century. Moreover, arranging the order of precedence would not always have been a simple affair. Unless the guests invited were a duke and duchess, an earl and a countess, a baron and a baroness, and a baronet and his wife, it was likely that the hostess would have had to make some sort of discerning judgement regarding the respective ranks of her guests.

In the earlier part of the nineteenth century, *A System of Etiquette* described two ways in which ladies and gentlemen might have proceeded into the dining room. According to one practice, the ladies would have gone into the dining room first, following the order of precedence. The gentlemen would have followed them afterwards, also respecting the order of precedence. Yet another practice was also detailed, whereby the gentlemen would have escorted the ladies into the dining room, and thus ladies and gentlemen would have gone in together. In this instance, the lady of the house would have led the way, escorted by the highest ranking gentleman. The lady of the house would have been followed by the highest ranking lady, who would have been escorted by the gentleman of the second highest rank. This pattern would have continued until the very end of the line, where the lowest ranking lady would have stood. She would have been escorted by the master of the house.

Subsequent guidance referred to the etiquette whereby ladies were escorted into the dining room by gentlemen. However, as previously mentioned, there seems to have been more than one way of going about this process. It was suggested in the late 1830s that when it was time to go into the dining room, the host should lead the way and should escort the highest ranking lady.[8] The hostess would then have gone next into the dining room, escorted by whichever gentleman had the greatest claim to the honour of acting in that capacity. Yet, only a few years later, *The Ladies' Pocket Book of Etiquette* put forward a different convention. It was said that the host should still lead the way into the dining room whilst escorting the lady of highest rank. However, the hostess would have gone into the dining room last, behind all of her other guests, and would have been escorted by the gentleman of highest rank. Here, it was also suggested that the rest of the guests would not normally have entered the dining room according to their order of precedence, but in whichever order happened to occur.

In contrast, during the second half of the century, *Mixing in Society* stressed the importance of the formal order of precedence. However, whilst the host was again instructed to lead the way with the lady of highest rank, the position of the hostess was somewhat in doubt. Although the standard practice was for her to go into the dining room last, it was thought that it might be more convenient if she were in the dining room before her guests, as this meant she would be present to help them find their seats. Towards the close of the century, *Manners and Rules of Good Society* advised that the proper etiquette for going into the dining room was for the host to lead the way with the lady of the most distinction, and for the hostess to go in last with the gentleman of highest distinction. The intervening guests would have gone into the dining room in accordance with the order of precedence.

Arranging this process of getting from the drawing room to the dining room would have required some forward planning on the part of the hostess. Even where the order of precedence was strictly observed, guests could not always have been expected, or perhaps relied upon, to know exactly where they fell in relation to everyone else in the room. And, in instances where the order of precedence was not followed, guests could still have been paired off by their hosts according to some design or other. Thus, the host or hostess would have intimated to the gentlemen which lady was to be entrusted to their chivalrous care at some point prior to going into dinner. Generally speaking, this would probably have been done with a reasonable amount of discretion once the guests were all assembled in the drawing room.

However, in order to get to the point where they could tell the gentlemen which ladies to escort, the pairing off would have had to be done. And, as hinted at before, this was not always an easy task. Indeed, with regard to the importance of forward planning and the order of precedence, hostesses were advised to consult works such as *Debrett's* or *Burke's* if they were expecting to receive particularly distinguished company.

Undistinguished – or, at least, untitled – company was not necessarily any easier to deal with. After all, even in instances where rank was otherwise equal, some order still had to be decided upon. So, the married could have been given precedence over the unmarried, and elder guests could have taken precedence over younger ones. Precedence could also have been given to the greatest stranger amongst the company.[9] Such an action would certainly have suggested that the stranger was a welcome addition to the party. There was also the option of pairing off guests according to which ladies or gentlemen were likely to prove pleasant dinner companions for each other.[10] Presumably, that would have required some careful consideration of the various guests' likes, dislikes and personalities.

A further courtesy to take into account was that a new bride might have been given precedence over all other ladies. However, it was suggested in the later years of the century that, by that point, this custom was normally only upheld in the country.[11]

In the process of escorting ladies into dinner, certain behaviour was expected of gentlemen. Gentlemen were instructed to remember that they were merely the gallant attendants to the ladies. It was always the lady who took precedence in this situation. Even offering the lady their arm was not a simple business. If they had to take any stairs to get to the dining room, then a gentleman would have ensured that the lady was on the side closest to the wall and thus furthest from the banister. If they were merely passing from one room to another, and so remaining on the same floor, then a gentleman would have offered his right arm to the lady he had the honour of escorting.

Let us take an example and illustrate it according to the advice which held sway at the end of the century. Mr and Mrs A, as we shall name them, were the obliging host and hostess. Their hypothetical dinner party was only a small one, but they were honoured to receive the company of a distinguished baronet and his wife. For the purposes of our example, they shall be called Sir B (addressed by his first name) and Lady B (addressed by her husband's surname).

Mr and Mrs A had also welcomed into their home a confirmed and somewhat elderly bachelor called Mr C. An amiable young bachelor, by the name of Mr D, was also in attendance. Mrs E, a widow of more mature years, was another guest who had consented to join the party. The last guest was a rather strong-willed spinster who delighted in being an old maid, and who had steadfastly refused every offer of marriage she had ever been made. Her name was Miss F. Also – so that we might add further colour to the picture – we shall say that Mr and Mrs A lived in a very respectably sized country house, and the drawing room and dining room were on the same floor. This would typically have been the case in a country house, but not in a town house.

Having already been informed who they were going to escort, the gentlemen would have known which lady was entrusted to their care when dinner was announced. As the drawing room and dining room were on the same floor, they would have offered their right arm to the appropriate lady. Mr A would have then led the way with Lady B. Mr C would have followed, acting as the escort to Mrs E. Then, the next in line would have been Mr D with Miss F. The last couple would have been Sir B and Mrs A.

In this brief example, the guests have been sent to dinner in accordance with the order of precedence and other similar considerations. Lady B would have taken precedence over all the other women as the wife of a baronet, and Mrs E would have taken precedence over Miss F owing to her age and marital status. Amongst the gentlemen, Sir B would have taken precedence because he was a baronet. As the elder of the remaining two gentlemen, Mr C would have been given precedence over Mr D.

Whichever approach was taken to sort out the order of precedence or the order for going into dinner – and it can be easily imagined that not everyone would have taken the same approach throughout the century, and that others would have stubbornly maintained their approach was the right one until the bitter end regardless of what anyone else thought – we can perhaps conclude that going to a nineteenth-century dinner party required rather more of the hosts than having enough food, and rather more of the guests than arriving with a decent bottle of wine to smooth over the proceedings. In that respect, it certainly makes planning a twenty-first-century dinner party appear a somewhat relaxed affair. Nevertheless, one way or another, the host, hostess and their guests would have somehow managed to get from the drawing room to the dining room. And this naturally brings us to the heart of the proceedings: the etiquette of the dining table.

Dining customs and habits changed significantly in the nineteenth century. Dinner moved from being served *á la française* to being served *á la russe*. Under the *á la française* style of eating, three courses would normally have been served. Each course would have been laid out on the table in turn, in a specific pattern, and multiple dishes would have been on offer.

A variety of soup, fish and meat dishes, as well as a collection of entrées, would normally have comprised the first course. The second course was rather more focussed on meat, serving up a selection of game, poultry, beef and so on. Dessert came with the third course where diners could have indulged themselves with fruits, nuts, jellies, ices and other treats.

Whilst grand establishments would have been able to provide numerous footmen to attend to the guests and make sure they did not miss out on any of the food, this method also ran the risk of abandoning diners in less opulent circumstances to shift for themselves. It was a style of eating that had the potential to leave a lady or gentleman disappointed, if their favourite dish was far away at the other end of the table. It is also not difficult to picture how such a dinner might have descended into chaos.

Dining *á la russe* was perhaps a move towards a simpler and more efficient way of eating. Under this method, the dishes were laid out on the sideboard instead of the table, and servants brought the food round to the guests in turn. Only fruits were placed on the actual dining table. The risk of missing out was greatly reduced. And whilst fewer dishes were served during each course, the number of courses on offer increased instead.

At the beginning of the century, it was suggested that the seating might be arranged in such a way as to sit the ladies at the top end of the table, with their places allotted according to the order of precedence.[12] Gentlemen would then have sat in a like fashion, but at the lower end of the table.

In the middle years of the period, it was said that the lady of the house would often have sat at the head of the table, with the gentleman of highest rank on her right and the gentleman of the second highest rank on her left.[13] The master of the house would then have sat at the bottom of the table, with the two ladies of highest rank on either side.

Alternatively, the host and hostess could have sat on opposite sides in the middle of the table.[14] This placed both the hosts and the guests of the most consideration at the centre of the gathering.

However, as the century was drawing to a close, advice suggested that the hostess should have sat at the top of the table with the gentleman who had taken her into dinner – and thus the highest ranking gentleman – sitting on her left.[15] The host would once more have sat at the bottom of the table with the lady he escorted – the lady of highest rank present – sitting on his right.

We can again see the influence of the order of precedence, but hostesses were also advised to try and keep apart guests who they thought might prove disagreeable to each other. Perhaps the desire to avoid awkward dinner party arguments is something which transcends time. It was also thought best to sit husbands and wives separately, although we shall assume this was to open up the company, rather than to avoid lovers' quarrels. As well as this, it was thought best to keep apart gentlemen who were engaged in the same profession, so as to prevent them from falling into a lengthy conversation on their particular shared interest.

When considering the etiquette of behaviour at the dining table, it is probably best to consider conversational etiquette before anything else. After all, having just mentioned the importance of keeping sparring partners apart, it seems a suitable place to mention that ladies and gentlemen were advised to keep their discourse during dinner polite and civil. Ladies and gentlemen were particularly instructed to avoid discussing religion and politics.

Conversation was not the only behaviour which etiquette manuals addressed. Some gave strict instructions to ladies and gentlemen about how they should behave when they had finally sat down. Advice given in the second half of the century decreed that, upon taking her place at the dining table, a lady would have moved her piece of bread and put it on her left-hand side. She would also have placed her napkin across her knees. Additionally, a lady would have removed her gloves and placed them on her lap, along with her fan and handkerchief. In a similar fashion, upon taking his seat, a gentleman would also have put his napkin across his knees and put his bread in its proper place.

Bread was not an item of food which was lacking in controversy. If cut according to the strictures of etiquette manuals, the bread would have been between 1 and 1½in thick. However, some felt that delicate, fancy rolls were more fitting for a dinner party. A lady or gentleman would have broken their bread with their hands when they wanted to eat it. It would have been thoroughly ill-bred of them to have cut it with a knife.

Of course, even if a lady or gentleman had managed to sit down and handle their bread correctly, their dining dilemmas did not end there. Taking and consuming fish and soup according to the proper etiquette was a further task faced by ladies and gentlemen at a dinner party. These constituted some of the first dishes of a dinner.

Perhaps reflecting the shift that had occurred between dining *á la française* and *á la russe* was the guidance given by *Mixing in Society* in the second half of the century with regard to the serving of fish and soup. Readers were advised not to serve fish and soup at the same time, as this was an old-fashioned habit. However, a greater offence was to ask guests to choose between fish or soup, which was thought to be a terribly dated custom. Soup and fish were to be treated as separate courses, and it was felt that most people preferred to have their soup first, followed by their fish.

It may also be possible to see this shift in dining habits in some advice given in the 1830s. Here, it was said that bowls of soup would be sent round to the guests once they were all seated.[16] However, if a guest preferred to have fish instead, they were advised to pass the soup along to their neighbour without comment. This demonstrates the dining habit – of having either soup or fish – that *Mixing in Society* had declared to be completely passé. This also underlines once more that etiquette advice changed during the century.

Ladies and gentlemen would, if following the demands of etiquette, have eaten their soup from the side of their spoon. It was thought unseemly to blow on one's soup to cool it down, if it was too hot. Slurping one's soup was also deemed highly improper.

For the greater part of the century, etiquette manuals instructed that fish was to be eaten with a silver fork and a piece of bread. The bread was held in a lady or gentleman's left hand, and the fork in their right. A knife was not supposed to be used. However, in the later decades of the century it was advised that fish should either be eaten with two silver forks, or with a silver fish knife and fork.[17] By the end of the century, the advice was that fish ought to be eaten with a silver fish knife and fork.[18] It was explained that the overwhelming custom had been to eat fish with a fork and piece of bread, and that this practice was indeed so popular that some still maintained it. However, it was said that the fashion for eating fish with two forks had been short-lived.

The etiquette of taking wine was also linked to the etiquette of eating one's fish and (or) soup. A gentleman would have been very remiss, if he asked a lady to take wine before she had finished her fish or soup. Indeed, after this portion of the meal was completed, someone sitting near to the hostess was supposed to ask her to take wine, as a hint to the rest of the company that wine taking was now acceptable.

Taking wine was the custom of two people drinking their wine at the same time. When taking wine, it was not necessary to say anything. One simply needed to catch the other person's eye and bow politely. If a lady or gentleman was asked to take wine, it would have been thought highly rude of them to refuse. However, it was not necessary for a lady or gentleman to drink a large amount of wine. It was thought perfectly acceptable to take a small sip, or to simply bring one's glass to one's lips. However, taking wine in this way was a custom which was on the wane through the nineteenth century. It was eventually declared to be completely out of fashion.

Yet, as well as understanding the practice of taking wine, ladies and gentlemen would have benefitted from being aware of some additional etiquette surrounding the serving and drinking of wine. In the late 1840s, *The Etiquette of Fashionable Life* explained that sherry and champagne were normally drunk during dinner. Madeira, claret and port were usually served afterwards. Certain wines could also be linked to certain dishes. According to advice given later on in the century, sherry was often served with soup.[19] Claret was served with red meat.[20]

Punch was thought to be a good accompaniment for turtle, and champagne for whitebait.[21] Port was served with game, but was also offered as an accompaniment to cheese.[22]

Furthermore, it would have been highly indicative of poor taste to speak of 'sherry wine' or 'port wine'. It was the sort of thing that would have made any well-bred individual shudder. The drinks were 'sherry' and 'port', nothing more and nothing less. Downing a glass of wine, if such a vulgar turn of phrase may be excused, would have displayed a shocking lack of table manners.

However, there were many more distasteful practices than this to be avoided and plenty of good habits to be cultivated. That was the impression given by etiquette manuals, at least. The ensuing paragraphs can perhaps best be read as a compendium of little nuggets of advice given to ladies and gentlemen at various points over the course of the century, all with the intention of enabling them to display the very best of manners.

To begin, a lady or gentleman would have known not to wipe their plate with their napkin at the start of a dinner. It would have been incredibly rude of them to imply that their hosts had provided a plate which was anything other than spotlessly clean. Equally, sniffing or otherwise examining the food on the end of their fork suggested they feared their hosts had provided rancid food. Of course, the hosts would not have done this.

Out of a mistaken sense of politeness, some ladies and gentlemen avoided taking the last piece of a dish. However, in seeking to be polite, they risked giving offence. Such an act intimated that they thought their host was unable to refill the dish.

Eating very quickly was also ill-bred. A lady or gentleman eating in such a manner risked leaving the other diners with the impression that it had been a long time since their last meal. Additionally, picking one's teeth at the dining table was considered to be a display of vulgarity that was best avoided. A lady or gentleman would also have known better than to talk with their mouth full. Sitting so far back from the table as to allow crumbs to be scattered all over the floor was thought to be a display of bad manners as well. Additionally, ladies and gentlemen were told that knives were for cutting, never eating. It was the height of bad manners to put food in one's mouth with a knife.

Advice was also given telling ladies and gentlemen how to eat certain foods. So for example, sauce was supposed to be poured on the side of the plate, not over the food. Guidance given in the 1830s suggested that peas were supposed to be eaten with a spoon.[23] Then in the second half of the century, ladies and gentlemen were told to eat them with a fork. Similarly, it was first thought best to use a spoon to eat tarts and puddings. However, it was later suggested that tarts and puddings should only be eaten with a spoon if it was not possible to eat them with a fork.[24] Jellies and blancmanges were also supposed to be eaten with a fork.[25]

A manual from the 1870s advised that cheese was another item that was best consumed with the aid of a fork.[26] However, later advice said that cheese was never eaten in that way. Instead, it was supposed to be cut with a knife and placed on small pieces of bread or biscuits. A lady or gentleman would then have picked the piece of bread or the biscuit up with their left hand – holding it between finger and thumb – in order to eat their cheese. However, it was felt that ladies, and sometimes more specifically young ladies, would rarely have eaten cheese at a dinner party.[27]

Hosts and hostesses were urged not to force food upon their guests. Whilst it was acceptable to maybe recommend or suggest something, putting one's guests in a position where they were effectively obliged to eat something which they might severely dislike was a poor show of hospitality.

One of the final matters to consider is the division of ladies and gentlemen. After the meal was finished, the ladies would have retired to the drawing room. The gentlemen would have remained in the dining room, before rejoining the ladies later on. According to advice given in the first half of the century, when the time came for the ladies to retire to the drawing room, the hostess would have risen from her seat at the table.[28] This would have acted as a signal to the other ladies that it was time for them to move into the drawing room. Of course, some sort of civility had to be shown to the departing ladies. In the

1860s, *Etiquette for All* suggested that the gentlemen would have escorted the ladies to the door as they had escorted them to the dining room before dinner.[29] Yet, guidance given in the later years of the century suggested a different practice. Here, it was felt that the hostess should have given the signal to retire by bowing to the lady of highest rank. This lady would then have risen and led the way from the room, with the ladies leaving in accordance with the order of precedence in which they had arrived. The hostess would have been the last to depart. The gentlemen would have stood, but would not have escorted them. The gentleman nearest the door, or perhaps the host, would normally have opened it for them.

The gentlemen would have remained in the dining room to enjoy each other's company and the host's wine. They were nevertheless admonished to exercise restraint and to not reappear before the ladies in a less than presentable state.

In the final decades of the century, it was stressed that gentlemen should not remain in the dining room for too long. Gentlemen were instructed that they were not – as had apparently been the case previously – to linger over their wine for more than an hour. If the gentlemen smoked, it was said that they would only do so after they were finished with the wine.[30] No gentleman would have ruined his wine by smoking at the same time as drinking. Such conduct towards wine was, it seems, unthinkable in refined circles.

Of course, as we now come to the close of a dinner party, the last major point of etiquette to consider was the manner in which guests left. Ladies and gentlemen were supposed to avoid breaking up the party, and so were advised to withdraw as discreetly as possible and without taking their leave. If their departure was a marked one, they ran the risk of reminding the other guests of the late hour, or of some other consideration, and of the master and mistress then having to witness their guests scrambling for the exit. However, towards the close of the century, guests were advised to take their leave of the hostess.[31]

It was also an important mark of civility for guests to acknowledge the dinner in some way after the event. In the 1830s, it was suggested that ladies and gentlemen should leave a card for the lady of the house the day after the dinner, or at the earliest possible time after that.[32] Later manuals advised that guests should pay a call or leave a card within a week of the dinner.

Some Principal Points of Politeness

- If invited to a dinner, a lady or gentleman would have responded without delay.
- Responses to invitations would have been addressed to the lady of the house.
- Punctuality was of the utmost importance.
- As a general rule, the guests would have proceeded to the dining room following the order of precedence.
- Whilst dining customs changed throughout the century, some basic manners included eating with one's mouth closed and not racing through one's dinner.
- It was polite to pay a call or leave a card soon after the dinner.

CHAPTER SIX

Some Remarks on Appropriate Ballroom Behaviour

There is something about a ball, some sense of fairytales and magic and romance, which cannot help but capture a person's imagination. However, this chapter has sadly got nothing to say about lost shoes and chivalrous princes. The image that we are trying to recreate here is not one of a happily ever after from the closing pages of a novel, but instead a piece of nineteenth-century life. Looking at the guidance given in etiquette manuals over the course of this era, we shall try and piece together some of the experience of what it would have been like to attend a ball during this period.

Naturally, the initial matter to which we must turn our attention is that of dancing. In this, we shall first consider which dances would have featured at a nineteenth-century ball. The second point we will explore is, of course, the etiquette advice which was attached to those dances.

The quadrille was a dance which held sway in ballrooms throughout the decades. Country dances were popular at the beginning of the century. However, as the period wore on, other dances such as the polka came to the fore. Yet, even as the century drew to a close, it was said that country dances still featured at private balls in the countryside.

One dance which generated no small amount of comment was the waltz. The waltz rather shook up the nineteenth-century dance scene, as it enabled a scandalous degree of improper personal contact between ladies and gentlemen. It was thought to be more than a little unseemly. And, whilst the shock did gradually wear off, it seems that the sense of scandal still lingered for some. Even in the second half of the century, *All About Etiquette* suggested that it might be more fitting to dance the waltz amongst a small gathering of family and close friends, rather than in a crowded ballroom. And, by that point, the waltz was acknowledged as an established favourite.

The manner in which a lady or gentleman danced was also important. Throughout the century, ladies and gentlemen who did not know a dance were exhorted to abstain from attempting it in a ballroom. Indeed, a manual for gentlemen advised its readers that it was bad manners to go to a ball if they could not dance.[1] It was not fair to risk embarrassing their partner with their poor dancing.

Ladies and gentlemen were further advised to dance without affection or stiffness. Their movements were instead supposed to be characterised by ease and grace. It was also thought that they should avoid dancing with studied neatness. As a number of etiquette manuals said, it did not do to dance with the air of a dancing master, because that was not the same thing as dancing with the air of a gentleman.[2]

There were some additional bad habits which ladies and gentlemen were cautioned to avoid. In particular, gentlemen were instructed to lead their partner in a dance, not drag them through it. Ladies were told to avoid boisterous behaviour and not to romp about the ballroom. Such conduct was apparently indelicate and unladylike.

However, whilst it was all well and good knowing the etiquette of how to dance, a lady or gentleman would also have needed to be conversant in the etiquette of the ballroom. Broadly speaking, there were two types of balls in the nineteenth century. These were public balls and private balls. There were differences between them, and they had their own expectations of etiquette.

A public ball – and the clue is perhaps in the name – was a ball open to the public. However, a lady or gentleman would have needed to have a ticket and obtaining one was not always an easy affair. For example, receiving a voucher for admittance to Almack's Assembly Rooms was no small matter. To gain a voucher here, a lady or gentleman would have had to have the social standing to pass muster with the Lady Patronesses, who set the bar rather high.

But, broadly speaking, it was thought that ladies and gentlemen ran the shocking risk of mixing with all and sundry when they attended public balls. This was particularly the case amongst public balls held for the middle classes as it was thought that, when it came down to it, almost anyone could gain entry. Readers were advised to avoid being seen at such balls too frequently, especially if they generally moved in more elevated social circles. Instead, it was thought better to seek out Assembly Rooms which were run under the patronage of the leading people within the locality. In the early years of the century, ladies were advised more generally to avoid attending public balls, or indeed any public entertainment or place, too often.[3] It was said that if they bestowed their presence upon the public with too much regularity, the value of their presence would be lessened.

When attending a public ball, a lady or gentleman would have avoided arriving too early. That was, of course, unless they had managed to gain entry to a place like Almack's. Around the middle of the century, *The Etiquette of Fashionable Life* suggested that 10 o'clock in the evening was the usual time to arrive at a public ball. A few decades later, *All About Etiquette* said that 10 or 11 o'clock in the evening was an appropriate time.

Upon arriving, it would have been good practice for a lady or gentleman to check the rules of the Assembly Room, in case the Assembly Room had some by-law or other with which they needed to familiarise themselves. If a gentleman was escorting a lady, he would have taken her to find a seat. He might also have been given a card listing the order of dances for the evening, with blank lines on the reverse where he would be able to note down his partner for that dance. After all, dancing was a rather important part of a ball. And, in order to dance, a lady or gentleman would have needed to obtain a partner. This brings us – really quite neatly – to the next point of etiquette for public balls.

For the greater part of the century, the Master of Ceremonies played a central role in pairing off ladies and gentlemen in a public ballroom. Simply put, the Master of Ceremonies acted in lieu of a host or hostess and was marked out by some badge of office, perhaps a sash or bow. The Master of Ceremonies might also have been assisted by stewards.

If a gentleman wished to dance with a lady, with whom he was not acquainted and had no mutual acquaintance in common, then he could have applied to the Master of Ceremonies to carry out an introduction. More generally, any lady or gentleman who wanted to dance but did not have a partner could have applied to the Master of Ceremonies to rectify the situation.

In the later years of the century, the role of the Master of Ceremonies seems to have diminished. He was instead replaced by a number of stewards, who were able to undertake any necessary or desired introductions between ladies and gentlemen. However, it was felt that, wherever possible, an introduction should have been made by a mutual acquaintance.

The importance placed upon having a proper introduction was very great indeed. Ladies were advised that they should never dance with a gentleman who had not been properly introduced to them. *Mixing in Society* even suggested that if a lady was asked to dance by a gentleman who had not sought an introduction, then she should make reference to his breach of etiquette when she declined. Rather than pleading fatigue or some other excuse, it was better for her to say that she would be happy to dance with him, if he would only obtain an introduction. That way, there could be no accusation of impropriety levelled at her for seeming to excuse or overlook his poor conduct. Gentlemen were also sternly told, in no uncertain terms, to expect nothing but a cool rejection if they behaved in such an ill-bred manner.

However, if a gentleman sought a proper introduction and then asked a lady to dance, she would have been obliged to accept. There was very little she could have done to escape the offer, unless she was indisposed or already had a prior engagement. Indeed, *The Etiquette of the English Ballroom* stated in the first half of the century that if a lady simply declined to dance with a gentleman, she would not have been allowed to join the next dance and might in some instances have been forced to stop dancing for the rest of the evening.

It seems that this obligation upon ladies to accept partners was not always considered fair or kind. Any gentleman with a passing knowledge of etiquette could have obtained an introduction to a lady, but that passing knowledge did not mean that he was an appealing partner for the lady in question. The lady might have thought that his manners were arrogant or foolish. There might have been many reasons why she wanted to reject his offer. And yet the lady could have found herself, owing to her own sense of good conduct and her knowledge of the rules of etiquette, consenting to dance with a gentleman she would have preferred to refuse. Indeed, some manuals advised gentlemen to take it on the chin and rise above being offended if they asked a lady to dance and she politely declined, and they then saw her dancing with a different man.[4] They pointed out that it was entirely possible that she might, without spite or malice, have simply preferred to dance with someone else.

Another point of etiquette to consider at a public ball was the offer of refreshments. At the conclusion of a dance at a public ball, a gentleman was supposed to offer the lady he had danced with refreshments. However, whether or not a lady accepted this offer was something of an etiquette conundrum. Some felt that ladies should see what the highest ranking ladies did, and then allow that to guide them in their answer.[5] Others felt that a lady should always decline, and only accept refreshments from her father, brother or an established acquaintance.[6]

A private ball would have been governed by different rules of etiquette, although some similarities can be seen. Naturally, as the ball was private and not public, invitations had to be issued. Given that there is never a dull moment when exploring nineteenth-century etiquette, the etiquette of invitations raises a number of interesting points for consideration.

What was thought to be a proper amount of notice between the issuing of invitations and the date of the ball seems to have varied throughout the century. There was some suggestion that invitations should have been issued a week to ten days in advance of the ball, or that this was the minimum amount of notice to give. However, other manuals advised that invitations should be sent out three weeks to a month beforehand.

The form of the invitation was very much orientated around the lady of the house throwing the ball, i.e. the hostess. The invitations would have been issued in her name only – by which is meant, she was the one extending the invitation – and replies would have been addressed to her as well.

With regard to invitations, there is a further point of etiquette which must be considered. It was thought to be terribly rude to be slow in replying to an invitation. In what can perhaps be interpreted as an extension of the etiquette of replying to dinner invitations, a response needed to be sent quickly. However, it would have been acceptable for a lady or gentleman to delay sending their answer when they were obliged to decline an invitation to a ball. After all, and as *Etiquette for Gentlemen* pointed out, if an invitation was received and then refused with the very next post, it might have looked as though the invitee did not want to go to the point of not wanting to set foot in the hostess' house, rather than that they were unfortunately prevented from attending owing to other engagements or extenuating circumstances.

There were some arrangements which hosts and hostesses were advised to make for the comfort and enjoyment of their guests. So, for example, it was felt that a particular room should be set aside for the use of any female guests. Ideally, this room would have been furnished with coat stands, looking glasses and attendants to aid ladies with their cloaks, hair and dresses. Another suggestion was that the cloaks should be ticketed, with a copy of the ticket being given to the owner. That way, when a lady came to leave, there would have been no difficulty for her in retrieving her cloak even if the ball had been a very large one.

When they arrived at a ball, the first duty of a lady or gentleman would have been to present themselves to their hostess. According to *Manners and Rules of Good Society* from the later years of the century, if there was a party of guests then the ladies were supposed to lead the way when entering and any accompanying gentlemen were supposed to follow behind them. It would not have been the proper etiquette for ladies and gentlemen to enter arm in arm.

As we have previously mentioned with reference to public balls, dancing was very much the order of the day. A ball would usually have been opened by the hostess, but if for any reason she could not undertake this duty, the host would have asked the lady of highest rank to dance with him. They would then have opened the ball instead.

The etiquette of obtaining and declining a partner is a further aspect of ballroom conduct which must be discussed. Where introductions were needed in a private ballroom, these were generally undertaken by the host, hostess or another member of their family. Again, a lady was obliged by etiquette to agree to dance with a gentleman, unless she could claim a prior engagement. Indeed, it was suggested in a manual from the middle years of the century that if a lady declined to dance with a gentleman, then she would have to sit out for that set.[7] Additionally, in a private ballroom, it was not always possible to avoid dancing with a gentleman because an introduction had not taken place. Whilst it would have been distinctly odd behaviour for a gentleman to ask a lady to dance without seeking an introduction first, a lady would have been under more than a little pressure to agree anyway, simply because his invitation from the hosts afforded the gentleman with a stamp of respectability. To decline might have been considered an insult to the host and hostess, as it implied that the lady supposed they had invited someone who was anything less than perfectly honourable. Of course, as we have already discussed, not everyone felt that this obligation upon ladies to accept dancing partners was the fairest or most reasonable rule of etiquette to hold sway in a ballroom.

We can also now consider how a request to dance might have played out differently depending on whether or not it had been made in a public or a private ballroom. Let us suppose that our gentleman in this instance was called Mr A. Whilst we shall not claim that Mr A was in anyway evil or devoid of basic morality, we shall say that his manners were somewhat lacking. He gave off a distinct air of arrogance and self-importance. The lady in this scenario was Miss B. Miss B perceived Mr A's arrogance and self-importance and did not wish to become acquainted with him, or indeed have anything to do with him. Feeling himself above the rules of etiquette, Mr A decided to ask Miss B to dance without seeking an introduction. In a public ballroom, Miss B could have coldly sent him on his way. In a private ballroom, she may well have felt herself obligated to endure his company.

When we imagine what a private ball might have been like for ladies and gentlemen in the nineteenth century, there are additional facets of etiquette and experience which we should take into consideration. For instance, with regard to the dance cards mentioned in relation to public balls, *The Etiquette of Fashionable Life* felt that it was more appropriate at private balls for a gentleman to refrain from making plans to dance with a lady until the next dance had been called.

As when dancing at a public ball, ladies and gentlemen at a private ball would most likely have found themselves to be in need of some refreshment during the course of the evening. At a private ball, a room might have been set aside for refreshments so that any dancers requiring sustenance could make their way there when needed. Alternatively, the refreshments could have been handed around if it was not possible to use a separate room.

When leaving a private ball, the etiquette was similar to that of a dinner party. It was thought best to leave as quietly and unobtrusively as possible, so as to avoid the risk of sending everyone else running home as well. However, in the later years of the century it was said that this rule applied to acquaintances and not intimate friends.[8] Or at least, it was suggested that this was the case for balls thrown in London.

Amongst the recommendations given to guests and hostesses with regard to the etiquette of leaving balls, one piece of advice from *Mixing in Society* from the 1870s stands out as particularly worthy of note. The author observed that guests, when departing from a ball, often struggled to secure a cab to take them home. It was suggested that if a hostess did not have more than one manservant, then she should instruct a policeman to stand on the pavement with a lantern, so that her guests would be able to procure transport with greater ease. She was also advised to notify a nearby cab stand that she would be holding a ball, so that the cab drivers would endeavour to be close by.

Lastly, and once more echoing the etiquette expected of ladies and gentlemen after a dinner party, guests at a private ball would have left a card with their hostess or paid a call at her place of residence within a week of the event.

In addition to the etiquette suggestions made for public and private ballrooms, there are other, more general, points about good and bad ballroom behaviour to consider. These will be explored here as something of a compilation of hints, tips and stringent warnings.

It was considered very bad form to get into an argument in a ballroom. A manual from the 1820s suggested that where a disagreement arose in a public ballroom, the two offending parties should leave with the Master of Ceremonies and not return until they were reconciled.[9]

Furthermore, whilst there has been plenty of advice with regard to finding a dancing partner, it must be said that husbands and wives would not normally have danced together. That is, at any rate, according to some advice given in the second half of the century.[10]

Additionally, going to a ball would most likely have been a marvellous excuse, for those so inclined, to dress up. And dress was another important point of etiquette. It was simply not on to turn up improperly attired. For instance, it would have been highly improper to appear without gloves. The colour was also a matter of some importance. As a general rule, a lady or gentleman could have worn gloves which were white or some other pale hue, but black gloves would have always been absolutely unacceptable. In a manual dating to the late 1840s, it was said that a fashionable gentleman would mainly have worn black to a ball, with a black neckerchief and a white waistcoat.[11] Ladies were advised during the second half of the century that ball gowns were best made out of light and airy materials. A ball would also have provided a lady with the opportunity to wear some of her more luxurious apparel, such as lace and diamonds.

Young ladies were instructed not to talk or laugh loudly in a ballroom. As well as this, they were told that it was mean-spirited to form a huddle and talk and laugh when a stranger entered. Naturally, it was unthinkable for an unmarried lady to attend a ball alone. She would of course have been accompanied by her mother, a married sister or some other suitable female chaperone. However, this is not to say that there were no comments directed towards gentlemen. They were told to avoid showing partiality for one particular lady in a ballroom. It was thought to ruin the mood.

Some Principal Points of Politeness

- Generally speaking, a private ball was thought to be better than a public one.
- When throwing a private ball, the hostess could have issued the invitations as much as a month in advance. However, she could also have sent out the invitations only a week beforehand.
- Invitations would have been issued in the name of the hostess and replies would have been addressed to her as well.
- At a private ball, dancing would normally have been opened by the hostess.
- If a gentleman had asked a lady to dance, she would have struggled to refuse him.
- It would have been very wrong for a lady or gentleman to fail to wear gloves in a ballroom.
- It was also thought better for ladies and gentlemen to avoid dancing if they were unfortunately afflicted with two left feet, or simply had not learnt to dance.

CHAPTER SEVEN

A Few Comments Regarding Conversation and Correspondence

Two further matters of etiquette which demanded the attention of ladies and gentlemen were the regulation of their conversation and the management of their correspondence. These were matters which could not be ignored. After all, success in any matter often hinges on the attention paid to the finer details. If that is a maxim which holds true now, it is not implausible that it held true a few hundred years ago as well. To illustrate this, we can conjure the example of a lady who paid and returned her calls with strict regularity. So far, it seems as though this lady handled the task with perfect propriety. However, if her conversation during those calls was perceived as vulgar or impolite, those calls can hardly be classed as successful. Equally, if a gentleman received an invitation to dine, he could have been rightly pleased at the compliment paid to him. Yet if he failed to answer the invitation, that initial compliment could well have been the last.

With regard to the etiquette of conversation, there were some expectations of politeness which – if contemporary etiquette manuals are to be believed – ladies and gentlemen would have been well-advised to follow. And of course, we must first of all and once again return to the highly important matters of rank, precedence and the proper application of titles. When addressing another person in speech, a lady or gentleman would have needed to use the correct form of address. As discussed in the opening chapter of this book, this meant if a member of the upper classes was, for instance, speaking to a duke, they would have colloquially addressed him as 'Duke'. And again, if a gentleman was a baronet or knight, then he would have been addressed as Sir George or Sir Henry or whatever else his first name might have been. His wife would then have been Lady Smith or Lady Green or whatever else their surname might have been.

It was not only the titled who had to be addressed properly. So, as noted previously, *Manners and Rules of Good Society* instructed that an army officer should have been addressed as Captain Thompson or Major Porter, or, again, in whatever fashion was appropriate. However, if he married, his wife would only have adopted his surname to become Mrs Thompson or Mrs Porter. She would not have taken on his military rank as well, and so would not have been known as Mrs Captain Thompson or Mrs Major Porter. And, without wishing to be too repetitive, even when the only titles in use were those of Mr, Mrs and Miss, it was still important that they were used correctly. It would have sounded awfully vulgar for a wife to refer to her husband as Mr B, or Brown, for example. A wife was supposed to refer to her husband properly, which in this instance would have meant calling him Mr Brown.

In addition, when conversing with other ladies and gentlemen it was thought best not to address them by name too frequently. Using another person's name as a form of conversational punctuation would have been in remarkably poor taste. Similarly, when conversing with those fortunate enough to be titled, ladies and gentlemen were reminded that only servants ended every sentence with 'My Lord' or 'My Lady'. For a lady or gentleman to speak in a manner more commonly used by servants would most likely have sounded rather odd to any other ladies or gentlemen within hearing range.

It was also considered polite to add 'Sir' and 'Madam' when answering a question in either the affirmative or the negative. So, let us imagine that a lady had remarked to a gentleman of her acquaintance that the weather was very fine that day. Had he simply replied, 'yes', even we in our modern world might consider that to be a somewhat blunt answer. However, following the 'yes' with a 'Madam' would have been more polite, and then adding a comment about how the weather was remarkably pleasant indeed would have presumably improved his response considerably.

1. Tail coat, New England, United States, *c.* 1820. From the Los Angeles County Museum of Art.

2. Fashion plate (evening dress) by Rudolph Ackermann, London, England, April 1826.
From the Los Angeles County Museum of Art.

3. Woman's dress, England, *c.* 1818. From the Los Angeles County Museum of Art.

4. Fashion plate (evening dress) by Rudolph Ackermann, London, England, December 1815. From the Los Angeles County Museum of Art.

5. Woman's dress, England, *c.* 1830. From the Los Angeles County Museum of Art.

6. Fashion plate (promenade dress) by Rudolph Ackermann, London, England, 1 December 1816. From the Los Angeles County Museum of Art.

7. Woman's bag (reticule), England, *c.* 1840. From the Los Angeles County Museum of Art.

8. Fashion plate (walking dress) by Rudolph Ackermann, London, England, June 1814. From the Los Angeles County Museum of Art.

9. Woman's bonnet, England or United States, late 1850s. From the Los Angeles County Museum of Art.

10. Fashion plate (walking dress) by Rudolph Ackermann, London, England, August 1814. From the Los Angeles County Museum of Art.

15. Woman's dress (wedding), United States, 1894. From the Los Angeles County Museum of Art.

16. Frock coat and trousers, Northern Ireland, *c.* 1852. From the Los Angeles County Museum of Art.

There were plenty of other tenets of conversational etiquette which a lady or gentleman would have borne in mind. Or at least, it is likely that they would have done so, if they wanted to follow polite etiquette. When in conversation, a lady or gentleman would have endeavoured to pay attention and to appear interested in what other people were saying. It did not matter if someone was exceedingly dull and boring. The conversational failings of another person would not have been an excuse for rudeness. Avoiding heated exchanges was also advised. If there was a point of disagreement, it was best simply to let it pass. If it was impossible to let the matter pass without remark, then the remark had to be delivered calmly, politely and without starting an argument.

So, let us suppose that Miss A – an engaging and lively young woman – was sat next to a young gentleman whom we shall call Mr B. There was nothing particularly wrong with Mr B, but we could perhaps say that his tastes and manners were rather more subdued than those of Miss A. Over the course of their conversation, Miss A felt that Mr B was droning on about nothing of interest and was at risk of sending her to sleep. However, it would have been very poor form for Miss A to start yawning. She would – we hope – have sought to appear interested and pleased to hear Mr B talk.

In this picture, further across the room, Mr C was talking to Mr D. Mr C was making some rather forceful remarks on the subject of politics, which Mr D could not accept. In such circumstances, it would seem that Mr D had two options. He could have chosen to ignore Mr C's remarks. Or, he could have replied to them in as neutral a manner as possible.

Of course, the above example only considers responses to other people's conversation. Ladies and gentlemen would naturally have had to monitor their own conversational conduct. A paramount principle of politeness was that a lady or gentleman would have refrained from boasting, and it was generally thought best for ladies and gentlemen to avoid talking about themselves as much as possible. So, whilst a lady may have been very pleased with her most recent efforts in needlework or watercolours, she would not have repeatedly pointed this out to everyone who happened to be acquainted with her. A gentleman might have been convinced that he had just purchased the best carriage in the county, but he would not have hosted a dinner party and spent the evening telling his neighbours all about it. Or, perhaps put more correctly, a lady or gentleman was not supposed to do those things.

On a similar note, a lady or gentleman was advised to avoid speaking at length on any topic. After all, they were supposed to be conversing with people, not making speeches at them. Thus, regardless of how passionately a gentleman might have wanted to hold forth on this matter of politics or that matter of business, he would have held himself back and allowed other gentlemen to have their say as well. Equally, however much he might have wanted to raise one point or another, he would not have done so if it meant interrupting someone else. He would have waited his turn. That was, as they say, the gentlemanly thing to do.

Additionally, when speaking, ladies and gentlemen would have avoided pulling faces and making gestures. A lady or gentleman would have simply spoken when they were engaging in a conversation. They were not supposed to have felt the need to turn a conversation into an audition for the stage. Ladies and gentlemen would also have resisted the urge to talk loudly. A conversation was meant to be a conversation, not a shouting match. It would have been an unpleasant, and perhaps even vulgar, display of poor manners for a lady or gentleman to have tried to dominate a conversation by being the loudest person present. By the same token, ladies and gentlemen would not have spoken so quietly that no one was able to hear them properly. They would also have avoided speaking too quickly.

Furthermore, ladies and gentlemen were instructed to refrain from using slang and provincial modes of speaking. Additionally, it would have been shockingly ill-bred for a gentleman to swear or use other improper language, especially in the presence of ladies and children. Another solecism which *Etiquette for Gentlemen* advised its readers to avoid was that of speaking in a language not understood by everyone present.

Unfortunately, the subject of conversational etiquette cannot be raised without mentioning scandal and gossip. Any good lady or gentleman would have refused to have any part in such undignified talk. They would not have listened to either scandal or gossip, and they would not have spread them.

Lastly, when selecting a topic for conversation, it would have been obvious to avoid the sorry subjects just mentioned above. However, another topic to avoid was a person's occupation. If a lady or gentleman found themselves in conversation with a physician or a clergyman or a barrister, they were advised not to ask them about medicine, religion or the law respectively. Engaging a gentleman in a conversation about his profession may have seemed natural, but it risked the implication that the lady or gentleman starting the conversation thought this was all the physician, clergyman or barrister in question could talk about.

Thus concluding our discussion of the etiquette of conversation, we must move on to the subject of correspondence. And a lady or gentleman would have needed to be able to correspond as well as they were able to converse. Writing letters could perhaps even be seen as a social duty, as it was a means of keeping distant relations and acquaintances informed of news and events. Ladies and gentlemen would have therefore needed to answer their letters in a timely fashion. Perhaps in a similar way to answering dinner invitations – where delay left the hostess wondering how many people she had to feed – leaving people without an answer to their letters was also impolite because the sender might have been anxious for a reply for some other reason.

For instance, let us say that Mrs E wrote to her close friend – whom we shall name Mrs F – and told Mrs F that she was feeling terribly under the weather. Mrs F, whose place of residence was a great distance from where Mrs E lived, was very concerned when she received this letter. She immediately responded with an urgent enquiry after her dear friend's health. If Mrs E had been slow to reply in this situation, poor Mrs F might well have become quite frantic with worry. And, during that time, Mrs E could have made a full recovery and been perfectly well. It is not hard to see how it would only have been considerate for a lady or gentleman to attend to their correspondence punctually.

When answering a letter, there were some simple matters to which a lady or gentleman would have paid attention. Or, as we have said before, they would have done so if they had chosen to follow the advice of etiquette manuals and wanted to make a good impression. So to begin, a letter had to be answered with a letter. However brief the initial note, if the sender had taken the time to write, the recipient ought to have taken the time to reply in the same manner. Had a lady or gentleman answered a written note verbally, such conduct might have been considered impolite or ill-bred.

Further to this, replying to a note on the same piece of paper as that note had originally been written was simply not sufficient. A lady or gentleman was advised to reply on a fresh sheet of paper. This sheet of paper was also supposed to be clean, plain and of good quality. Advice given in the second half of the century also elaborated upon this, suggesting that gilt edges and extravagantly coloured monograms were marks of vulgarity to be rigorously avoided. If a lady or gentleman had a monogram or crest printed upon their paper, they were advised to have styled it in a simple and unostentatious manner.

Assuming that there were no other formalities to take into account, such as a title of the peerage, a letter would most likely have been addressed to 'Sir' or 'Madam' if the recipient was not well known to the writer. Alternatively, 'Dear Sir' or 'Dear Madam' might have been used between individuals who were on warmer terms with each other.

A letter would often have been signed off with some expression of obedience. For instance, one gentleman might have styled himself as honoured to be the obedient servant of another gentleman. This was a polite courtesy, not an actual intimation that one person was beholden to another. However, in the later decades of the century, *Etiquette: What to Do and How to Do It* advised its readers that formal letters should close with either the expression 'Yours faithfully' or 'Yours obediently'. Of course, it is difficult to imagine that everyone – an obvious example being close friends and family – would have written to each other in the style outlined in this and the preceding paragraph.

Black ink was recommended for writing letters. Ladies and gentlemen were also instructed to write in neat, clear handwriting and to punctuate their letters properly. They were additionally told that remembering to date their letters was important. Let us imagine, for example, that a younger sister wrote frequently to her elder sister who had married and now lived many miles away. The younger sister failed to date her letters. For some unknown and unfortunate reason, a number of the younger sister's letters were once delayed. This meant that the elder sister later received a whole bundle of letters all at the same time. However, this meant that the poor elder sister, who presumably had many duties to attend to, was left piecing together her sister's news and assembling the letters into some sort of logical order. And the labour could have been easily avoided, had the younger sister taken the time to write the date on her letters.

With reference to the tone and content of letters, these would naturally have been dictated by the reason for writing and the relationship between the two correspondents. However, a lady or gentleman would have been taking a risk in writing something secret or controversial. After all, whatever a lady or gentleman's correspondent later said, it was impossible to be absolutely certain that they had burned the offending missive.

A further important piece of etiquette is that it would have been a serious breach of propriety for a young lady to correspond with a gentleman, unless he was a relation or they were engaged to be married. Indeed, in the second half of the century *All About Etiquette* warned young ladies that even if they wrote to a gentleman on the most mundane subject, an unscrupulous gentleman might use the letter against them and damage their reputation. And whilst it was permissible for a betrothed lady and gentleman to correspond, it was expected that both parties would have returned any letters exchanged between them if they broke off their engagement.

We have at last arrived at the final point of etiquette which we shall consider in relation to correspondence. And that is the issue that once a letter had been composed – legibly and with perfect propriety – it needed to be sealed. Envelopes were not commonly used before the 1840s, so in the earlier part of the century a completed letter would have folded and then sealed. A letter might have been sealed with wax or a wafer. A wafer was a mixture of gum and flour that stuck the pieces of paper together. If using sealing wax, *Etiquette for Gentlemen* from 1838 advised its readers to use red wax when writing to gentlemen and coloured wax when writing to ladies. Interestingly, this manual also advised readers to use envelopes when sending a reply to an invitation. In 1840, *The Ladies' Pocket Book of Etiquette* also felt that envelopes were more suitable when sending requests, congratulations and invitations. At the same time, ladies were advised to seal these envelopes with wax. A lady was not supposed to use a wafer. Indeed, in the second half of the century, it was declared outright that wafers were utterly obsolete and not to be used.[1]

Some Principal Points of Politeness

- When in conversation with another person, a lady or gentleman would have endeavoured to use the correct form of address.
- A lady or gentleman would also have sought to pay attention when another person was speaking.
- A lady or gentleman would have refrained from interrupting other people and from starting arguments with them.
- A lady or gentleman would have avoided boasting.
- A lady or gentleman would also have avoided talking at great length.
- It was important for a lady or gentleman to respond to their letters in a timely fashion.
- It was also important to write neatly, correctly and to put the date on letters.
- It was best to write letters on plain, good-quality paper.
- It would have been most improper for a young lady to write to a gentleman, unless he was either a relation or her betrothed.
- If a lady and gentleman ended their engagement, they were supposed to return any letters exchanged between them.

CHAPTER EIGHT

Some Advice Pertaining to the Employment of Domestic Servants

Many changes took place over the course of the nineteenth century, and a key change to bear in mind here was the increased reliance of ladies and gentlemen upon servants. Tasks that many ladies or gentlemen would most probably have done for themselves at the start of the century were carried out by servants at the end of it. This alteration must be borne in mind, and once more reflects that the lives of ladies and gentlemen in 1800 would have been very different to the lives of their descendants in 1900. An additional point to consider is that whilst etiquette manuals exhorted employers to treat their servants properly, and of course some ladies and gentlemen would have done so, others would have treated their servants shockingly. We must therefore remember that just because advice was given, this does not mean that it was followed.

Before the etiquette of employing servants can be addressed, the business of hiring them must first be tackled. Naturally, a lady or gentleman could only have hired such servants as they could afford and as were appropriate for the size of their establishment. It would have been nonsensical for a husband and wife of modest means to have tried to engage the same amount of staff as a duke and duchess.

The running of an establishment often fell to the lady of the house. A lady on the look-out for a new servant could have chosen to use the services of a respectable registry office. However, it was suggested that it was better for a lady to hire her servants on the basis of a personal recommendation. This would have given her the reassurance that her servants came with a personal stamp of approval from someone she knew. And, naturally, a lady would not have known someone who was not respectable. Local tradespeople were said to be a good source of information, as were friends and acquaintances.

Isabella Beeton's *The Book of Household Management* also advised ladies to be cautious of hiring servants on the basis of a written reference. In what we might perhaps view as an amusing act of nineteenth-century social espionage, it was suggested that ladies attempt to obtain an interview with a potential servant's former mistress. In this way, a lady would have been able to scout out what sort of establishment her prospective servant was accustomed to, and to see if the servant had been set a bad example by a mistress with a disorderly and badly run household.

When it came to hiring servants, ladies and gentlemen could have expected to get what they paid for. If they paid their servants poorly, then they were told to anticipate being served poorly in return. It was said that a good servant would look for a good position elsewhere, where they would be properly recompensed for their labour. A skilled butler, a thorough housemaid, an accomplished governess or indeed any other servant competent in their trade ought to have been a valued employee. If an employer did not recognise this, the servant in question was perfectly entitled to seek a new one who did.

Furthermore, in *The Women of England* from the first half of the century, ladies were advised to be upfront about the work they wanted their servants to perform. It was not fair for prospective employers to withhold details of expected duties from servants when advertising or interviewing for a role, and to then expect the new servant to be thrilled when they finally did find out about them. Therefore, a lady or gentleman would have made any extra or additional responsibilities clear in advance of engaging a servant for a position.

Of course, the responsibility of being a good employer did not end when a new servant took up their post. A lady or gentleman was supposed to treat their servants kindly and fairly. In addition, it was thought that a good master or mistress was served better by their servants than a bad one. The employer and servant relationship was in many ways reciprocal, and the employer got back what they put in.

We have already covered this with regard to wages. Likewise, if a master or mistress treated their servants unfairly, they could hardly have claimed to be truly surprised when their servants were sullen, lax in their duties or prone to packing their bags and leaving without warning.

In what could potentially be seen as an extension of this, etiquette manuals instructed ladies and gentlemen to speak courteously to their servants. They did not need to bark or shout, and nor did they need to speak haughtily or rudely. An instruction could be given to a servant following some sort of phrasing along the lines of a request. A direction to a servant, for example, could have been expressed in such as way as to suggest that the lady or gentleman in question would thank them – the servant – if they would bring them some refreshment.[1] The instruction, thus issued, could still have conveyed a tone of authority and the expectation that it would be dutifully fulfilled. However, it would also have been communicated in a manner far more civil and becoming to a lady or gentleman.

A lady or gentleman would also have held back from publically reprimanding their servants.[2] If they were displeased with the work of a servant whilst receiving visitors or entertaining company, a lady or gentleman would have waited and addressed it at a later time.

Moreover, whilst they might sometimes have found a fault that needed to be corrected, ladies and gentlemen would have recognised that all human beings made honest mistakes from time to time.[3] Further to this, employers were reminded to be reasonable in their expectations and requests.[4] For example, it would have been perfectly acceptable for a lady or gentleman to ask for a particular outfit to be made ready for an important occasion. However, it would have been completely unreasonable if, in the process of getting dressed, they announced they wanted to wear something else and became annoyed that it was being washed, or mended or was simply not immediately to hand.

A final point of etiquette to consider is the giving of references. To be concise, a lady or gentleman would have remembered that they had a duty to both the servant in question and any potential future employer. They would have been guided by fairness and truth. They would not have written a nasty reference out of spite, or a glowing one when it was not deserved.

Some Principal Points of Politeness
- It was advised that ladies should try and engage servants on the basis of a personal recommendation.
- Ladies and gentlemen were instructed to treat any servants they employed justly and fairly.
- They were supposed to pay their servants a good wage.
- They were also supposed to have reasonable expectations.
- If they had to give a former servant a reference, ladies and gentlemen were advised to be fair to both the servant in question and to any future employer that servant might have.

CHAPTER NINE

Courtship, Marriage and the Etiquette Thereof

It would certainly be nice to envision a happy couple driving off into the sunset in a brand new carriage, heading towards a sizeable and debt-free estate. However, as wonderful and romantic as that would be, that is not really the business at hand. We are not looking for tales of everlasting love in the nineteenth century. Rather, our focus is on recommended etiquette and conduct. Our interest is in how a lady or gentleman was advised to behave whilst their heart may or may not have been bursting with passionate adoration for another. And then, our interest is in the etiquette attached to the celebration of a wedding. Thus, in this chapter we shall explore the advice given with regard to conduct towards suitors and marriage, the act of proposing and of accepting an offer of marriage, and the instructions given for the form of weddings and post-wedding celebrations.

However, there are a two points which must be borne in mind. The first relates to the romantic happy ending mentioned above. Of course, ladies and gentlemen did marry for love in the nineteenth century. Yet, it must also be remembered that this would not necessarily have been the case for all ladies and gentlemen. And some ladies in particular may have faced a choice between marriage and permanent dependence upon their families. As well as this, marriage might have been a means of escaping serious financial hardship when few other options were available. For example, a lady without an inheritance, and without a family possessed of the means or inclination to support her, could well have seen marriage as a way of securing her future.

The second point, which must be mentioned, pertains to the

changes that marital celebrations underwent over the course of the nineteenth century. At the beginning of the century, weddings were normally quite small and private events. There may have only been a handful of guests. Under the Victorians, weddings grew to become rather more lavish affairs. The exploration of the etiquette of proposals and the etiquette of the marriage celebrations in this chapter reflects this change, as much of the advice is drawn from manuals dating to the second half of the century.

Before we leap into proposals and wedding planning, we should perhaps consider the advice given relating to the idea of marriage. For example, how a lady was supposed to approach the prospect of getting married and becoming a wife. Whilst such guidance cannot show us how people actually felt or behaved, it does provide something of an insight into attitudes and adds a little to our attempt to try and imagine life during the nineteenth century.

In the early years of the century, *Principles of Politeness* urged young ladies to be circumspect and discreet in their approach to love and marriage. With regard to marriage, they were cautioned that young ladies who were impatient to be married were likely to find themselves in an unhappy union. Love was also framed as an emotion which would cause a lady to feel embarrassed, owing to her modesty. It was said that a lady often did not fall in love before a gentleman. Instead, a lady would hold a good gentleman in high regard and would then perceive that he had formed an attachment to her. A lady would then feel gratitude for the attachment and her love would grow out of that gratitude. Additionally, when wrestling with feelings of love, young ladies were advised to conceal the emotion as much as they possibly could. If they wanted to divulge their feelings to another, they were advised to entrust their secret to someone who had only their happiness and best interests at heart, such as their mother, father or a doting brother.

These sentiments were echoed in the middle of the century. A young lady, if behaving according to the conduct prescribed in etiquette manuals, would have reflected seriously upon the possibility of love and marriage. She would have earnestly considered what she expected married life to be like, and what she thought constituted happiness in the married state.[1] As well as this, she would have gravely examined a prospective husband's moral character, and she would have turned to her parents for support and guidance.[2]

That importance was placed upon discreet conduct can be seen once again in the remonstrations of etiquette manuals against coquetry. Coquettish behaviour was decried as deplorable in a young lady and as an affront to everything that was right and proper. No young lady, who valued what it meant to be a lady, would have conducted herself in such a heinous manner as to engage in meaningless flirtations, or to toy with the affections of a decent and respectable gentleman in a calculated fashion. In what might perhaps be considered a similar line of thought, *The Mirror of Graces* stoutly declared in the early years of the nineteenth century that there was no such thing as a good-natured kiss, and that women who were tempted or induced into such behaviour often found that it ended very badly for them.

Taken together, the advice given in etiquette manuals could be seen to suggest that a certain amount of reserve, reticence and prudence was expected of ladies when considering love and marriage. Such an approach seems quite logical – if a little unromantic – if a person believed that the responsibilities of a wife and mother were not something to be undertaken lightly and when a lady's husband was supposed to be her companion and provider for life.

However, let us now suppose that a young woman – who had never engaged in coquetry and who had never conducted herself in a manner that was anything less than perfectly discreet – had gained the affection and esteem of a worthy and honourable young man. In these circumstances, there are a number of ways in which she might have acted depending upon the situation and her own feelings.

In the first instance, we shall imagine that, for one perfectly sound reason or other, the young lady did not wish the gentleman to pursue his affection. In fact, she desired him to fix his love upon another lady and to live a long, happy and emotionally fulfilling life with her instead. We shall also presume that the gentleman in question had not made any actual declaration of his love or intentions. Under these circumstances, a young lady would have sought to communicate her sentiments in the kindest and most humane way she could, so that the blow to the gentleman would have been as soft as possible. Thus, she might have asked a responsible friend to intercede on her behalf. Alternatively, she might have avoided, or subtlety shown that she wished to avoid, the gentleman's company. Another method would have been to communicate through her manner that she did not hold him in a different level of regard than any other gentleman of her acquaintance. These were all considered to be acceptable responses to the situation, suggested between the beginning and middle years of the nineteenth century.

In the next instance, we shall presume that a proposal of marriage had been made and that the young lady wished to decline it. Once again, etiquette demanded discretion on the part of the lady. If she received and rejected an offer of marriage, the best conduct would have been to remain silent on the subject. She would certainly not have allowed the information to become public knowledge to her friends and general acquaintance. All offers of marriage were supposed to be received with dignity and courtesy, regardless of whether or not a lady intended to turn them down. According to *The Etiquette of Love, Courtship and Marriage* from the second half of the century, the young lady could have chosen to refer the gentleman to her parents when she declined his offer of marriage. Her parents would then have been the ones to inform the gentleman of their daughter's decision.

Of course, a far more pleasing scenario to imagine would be one where the young lady returned the gentleman's love, accepted his proposal and their families and circle of acquaintance were all absolutely delighted with the match. However, even in that instance, and in the instance of the rejected proposal outlined above, there was a certain amount of etiquette attached to the act of proposing which should also be considered.

Firstly, advice given in the second half of the century felt that a gentleman should have obtained the permission of a young lady's parents or guardians before he made her an offer of marriage.[3] As the century drew to a close, it was suggested that this was no longer strictly necessary.[4] Nevertheless, although prior parental consent was not needed, it was thought wrong for a gentleman to propose to a lady if he knew her family would object to the union.[5] Also, upon receiving a positive answer from a lady, a gentleman was then supposed to apply to her father for his approval as soon as possible.[6] Secondly, and perhaps as an extension of this, secret courtships and clandestine elopements were strongly discouraged. They were even said to lead to unhappy marriages.

The third matter to be addressed is the form of a proposal. Whilst a gentleman might have proposed to a lady in person, it would also have been acceptable for him to ask for her hand in a letter. However, it was said that a young lady should not have answered such a letter without first showing it to her parents and consulting them on the matter.

As we said before though, the happiest outcome to picture is one where the lady and gentleman were very much in love, and their friends and family were very pleased to hear of their engagement. If we take that scenario and continue with the etiquette of what would happen next, we can now consider the jolly interlude between the proposal and the wedding ceremony.

Etiquette manuals dating from the second half of the century said that once a gentleman had had his proposal accepted, he was supposed to present his future bride with a ring. It was also normal for a gentleman to bestow other gifts upon his beloved as well. If a lady's parents did not consent to the giving of grander gifts, it would still have been permissible for the lady to accept flowers, which the gentleman could then have given as liberally as he liked.[7]

There were additional matters of behaviour to consider. According to *The Etiquette of Love, Courtship and Marriage*, ladies were supposed to be reserved in their behaviour towards their future husband and would have avoided over-familiarity. True love was not shown through great displays of affection, but was by its very nature quiet and modest. Whilst a betrothed lady and gentleman had to pay a suitable amount of attention to each other, conduct on both sides was supposed to be respectable and restrained.

Another part of the wedding preparations was the bridal trousseau. In the 1850s, *Bridal Etiquette* declared that the trousseau was supposed to supply the bride with plenty of the basic necessities of clothing to help see her through the early period of her marriage. It would have been filled with things such as underclothes, although bonnets and other outfits might have been added as well. However, the contents of the trousseau would naturally have been dictated by the means of the bride's parents. Where luxury was not possible, plain, simple and durable items were recommended instead.

Of course, the wedding day itself also had to be planned. It was the privilege of the bride to name the day. In the later years of the century, *Manners and Rules of Good Society* said that invitations should be despatched within two weeks of the day named for the wedding. The invitations were supposed to be issued in the names of both of the bride's parents.

Additionally, the bridal outfit would most likely have formed no small part of the wedding preparations. Like the trousseau – and indeed the wider wedding celebrations – the bride's wedding dress would have been dictated by her fortune and situation in life. However, the advice given by *Bridal Etiquette* in the middle of the century suggested that the appropriate colour for a bridal gown was always white. This was, at least, the case for first-time brides. Widows who were re-marrying might have decided that it was more fitting to choose a different colour. Indeed, some manuals went further and felt that it was not appropriate for a widow to wear white.[8]

A bride could have chosen to wear either a veil or a bonnet. The veil could have been made from a number of materials, such as Brussels or point lace, or simple tulle. If opting for a veil, then ladies were advised that it should be accompanied with a wreath of orange flowers. Orange flowers were also used to trim bonnets. However, etiquette manuals made additional and alternative suggestions for widows. For instance, it was said that a veil was more fitting for a young bride, whilst a widow might have felt it more prudent to select a bonnet.[9] This recommendation was also made to first-time brides of more mature years.[10] Again, some went further and said that a widow should simply not wear a veil at all.[11] Under this advice, a widow was also supposed to forgo wearing any orange flowers.

The bride could have chosen to be attended by bridesmaids, and she would have normally selected them from amongst her sisters, other relations or close friends. Although they were not supposed to be dressed in a similar style to the bride, it was considered appropriate for them to be dressed in white as well.[12] The position of chief bridesmaid would usually have been given to the bride or groom's eldest unmarried sister. However, it was also said that it was more correct for a widow to be married without bridesmaids.[13]

For the purposes of fairness and propriety in our exploration of etiquette, the clothing of the groom must also be mentioned. In the second half of the century, *Bridal Etiquette* suggested that a suitable outfit for the groom consisted of a black coat with black trousers and a white waistcoat.

With the trousseau ready, the invitations sent out and the happy couple suitably attired, we have reached the proper point to address the etiquette of the wedding day. On the appointed day, the guests were supposed to arrive before the bride. Indeed, this was not a time to be late. The bride's guests would have been seated on the left-hand side of the church and the groom's on the right.

The bride and groom would have travelled to the church separately. The bride would have gone to the church in her father's carriage, accompanied by her mother. If the bride's father was deceased then the carriage would have been provided by another close male relation. If the bride's mother was deceased then another close or married female relation would have accompanied the bride in her place.

The bride would have been met at the church door by the gentleman who was to give her away. This person would normally have been her father. The bride's father – or the gentleman acting in his stead – would have led the bride down the aisle and any bridesmaids would have followed behind them.

The Etiquette of Love, Courtship and Marriage remarked in the middle of the century that there was a custom amongst the middle classes for the groom to kiss the bride at the end of the wedding ceremony. However, it was said that this was not the custom amongst the best circles in society, and was consequently to be avoided. If the bride was to be kissed by anyone, it should have been elderly relations, doing so in congratulation.

The bride and groom would have departed from the church together, usually in the groom's own carriage or his father's carriage. They would then have repaired to the wedding breakfast or the wedding tea. These celebrations would generally have been hosted by the bride's parents. Whether the marriage ceremony was followed by a wedding breakfast or a wedding tea was dependent upon the time of the ceremony. In the last two decades of the century, it was said that afternoon weddings had become increasingly popular.[14] A later wedding meant a wedding tea, rather than a wedding breakfast.

The wedding cake was a prominent feature of both a wedding breakfast and a wedding tea, and advice from the 1850s felt that it was particularly fitting for the cake to be decorated with orange flowers.[15] After the cake had been cut, toasts would have been proposed. Toasts, in this instance, meant proposing a drink to someone's health. Advice from the middle of the century suggested that the first toast was supposed to be made by the oldest friend of the family, proposing a toast to the health of the bride.[16] Then, one of the groom's friends was supposed to propose a toast to his health. If the groom did not have any friends in attendance, then his father-in-law or another of his new relations should have made the toast instead.

According to advice given in the final decades of the century, the first toast could have been made by the gentleman of highest rank, the most distinguished guest, or the person who had known the newly married pair for the greatest amount of time.[17] They would have proposed that the assembled company drink to the health of the bride and groom. The groom would have then proposed a toast to the health of the bridesmaids. The final toast was proposed by the groom's father, to the health of the bride's mother and father. However, at a wedding tea, sometimes only the health of the bride and groom was toasted.[18] Indeed, as the century drew to a close, it was said that this was always the case.[19] It was also remarked that a bride and groom did not always attend a wedding tea.[20] If the bride and groom had had a later wedding, and then needed to make their departure for their wedding tour, there simply may not have been enough time. It was felt that wedding teas – and thus afternoon weddings – were more popular with grooms for this reason.[21]

After the drinking of the toasts, it would have been time for the bride to change from her wedding dress into an outfit which was suitable for travelling. The bride and groom would then have taken their leave. Leave-taking was supposed to be done as quickly and painlessly as possible, so that tears would be avoided.

Wedding tours were quite popular amongst the middle and upper ranks of society. These were taken immediately after the marriage. The length and destination of the tour would have been determined by the circumstances of the bride and groom. A richer couple would naturally have been able to afford a more extravagant wedding tour. Trips to the Continent were generally of a longer duration, perhaps three or four months.[22] If the couple remained closer to home the trip might have lasted three or four weeks instead.[23] It was said in the middle of the century that whilst in the past the bride and groom would frequently have been accompanied by a friend or two, the usual practice at the time was for them to go alone.[24]

Once the bride and groom had returned home and begun their married life together, there were still some points of wedding related etiquette to consider. So, for example, in the middle of the century *Bridal Etiquette* felt that it was perfectly appropriate for a recent bride to have some token of her new status in her attire when going to parties. She might have chosen to arrange some orange flowers in her hair, for instance. Also, a new bride might sometimes have been given precedence when going into dinner. However, as the century came to an end, it was said that this was an old-fashioned custom that was normally only observed in the countryside.[25] Of course, we have already remarked upon this in an earlier chapter.

One key piece of etiquette following the wedding was the sending of wedding cards. After their marriage, the bride and groom would have sent out their cards together. It was felt that upon his marriage, all of a gentleman's acquaintances came to an end, and they were only resumed if they were included in the sending out of the cards. This custom was apparently owing to a lack of discretion shown by bachelors when deciding who to admit into their acquaintance.[26]

Wedding cards might also have contained information about days on which the bride and groom would be 'at home' to receive callers. Alternatively, cards giving details of these days could have been sent separately. This might have been dependent on the circumstances. So, if the happy pair were planning a long jaunt in Europe, it may have been thought easier to send information about days to receive callers once they had returned home. This would have saved people from attempting to pay a call on one of the appointed days, only to find that the appointed day had become redundant, and the perhaps now slightly less happy couple were delayed on the other side of the Channel. However, other advice suggested it was simply customary to send wedding cards separately to 'at home' cards when the couple had completed their wedding tour.

On the particular days for receiving guests, callers would have been given wine and wedding cake, and it was generally a time to be pleased for the new couple. If the groom was unable to be present, perhaps owing to the demands of his profession, then *Etiquette, Social Ethics and the Courtesies of Society* recommended that an old family friend should stand in his place and that an apology should be made to callers. Regardless of whether or not the groom was present, the bride should have had someone there to support her, such as her mother, sister or another suitable person.

Newly married ladies and gentlemen might also have sent wedding cake at the same time as sending their wedding cards. In the 1840s, it was said that the former custom had been always to send some wedding cake with the wedding cards, although the practice was now on the wane.[27] Yet, as it was a custom still retained by some of the best families, it was a perfectly acceptable thing for the couple to do if they wanted to. In the 1850s, it was suggested that the custom of sending wedding cake was normally only maintained by those living in the country.[28] In those circumstances, where it was more difficult for people to see each other, the couple might have sent out pieces of wedding cake. Or, if they did have callers and could distribute the cake at home, wedding cake might then have been sent to more distant connections.

However, towards the end of the period, wedding cards were declared to be completely out of fashion.[29] Further to this, adding any details to marriage announcements printed in the newspapers about days the couple would be 'at home' to receive callers was thought to be very vulgar. In the final decade of the nineteenth century, the practice of sending wedding cake to friends was also said to be all-but obsolete.[30]

Some Principal Points of Politeness

- Ladies were advised to approach the prospect of marriage with a great deal of prudence.
- Although by the end of the century it was not strictly necessary for a gentleman to obtain the permission of a lady's father to propose, it was felt that it would be wrong for a gentleman to propose if he thought an objection was likely to be raised.
- If a gentleman proposed and was accepted, it was important for him to go to the lady's father as soon as possible to confirm his approval for the match.
- Secret courtships and elopements were generally discouraged.
- Once an engagement was confirmed, the gentleman would have presented his future bride with a ring.
- The bride had the privilege of naming the day of the wedding.
- The bride and groom would have travelled to the church separately, but would have left together.
- The wedding ceremony would have been followed by a wedding breakfast. However, an afternoon wedding would have been followed by a wedding tea.

CHAPTER TEN

Particular Hints for Ladies

In the nineteenth century, there were some matters of etiquette and conduct which were particularly addressed to ladies. These included the duties that came with managing a household and how a lady would go about ensuring she was well-dressed. However, the first matter we shall consider is what it meant to be a lady.

Through etiquette, we have explored many details of the lives of ladies and gentlemen. Etiquette has allowed us to examine customs and habits – for instance those of the ballroom and dining room – and has enabled us to try and imagine many aspects of nineteenth-century life. Additionally, we have been able to consider some physical elements of this period, such as ink and paper and cards. Yet, the next topic to which we shall turn our attention focusses on a further element of life and experience. Etiquette manuals also raised points about what it meant to be a lady, i.e. the qualities which they believed that a lady should have possessed. These qualities can also be viewed as personal qualities, as internal traits of character. Of course, it would have been perfectly possible for a lady to behave as though she had this or that quality, without actually being in possession of it. Nevertheless, the discussion of what it meant to be a lady – the points which were addressed to them and made about them – is certainly interesting for questioning and exploring the nineteenth-century world.

A number of positive qualities, or qualities which were presented as positive, were put forward as some of the hallmarks of a lady. An etiquette manual dating to the early years of the century placed some weight upon the importance of modesty in a lady.[1] It was not ladylike to want to be the centre of attention, and to want all eyes to turn towards oneself. A lady was supposed to have a retiring nature. Indeed, as the middle of the century approached, a further manual expressed the belief that boisterous behaviour was improper and unladylike.[2]

Let us suppose that there were two young ladies who were equals in birth, education and social standing. Perhaps they were both the daughters of respectable country gentlemen. Indeed, perhaps those two gentlemen were even neighbours. And we shall say that the first young lady was called Miss A and the second young lady Miss B, and that they both went one night to a ball thrown by a third, very generous neighbour. At this ball, Miss A spent the evening quite clearly seeking to draw attention to herself, whilst Miss B behaved in a more restrained manner. According to the etiquette guidance outlined above, we could conclude that Miss B had displayed more ladylike qualities than Miss A.

Further points were raised as well. Being quick to blush was said to be a good trait for a lady to have, as it demonstrated an innocent mind. Morality was put forward as a foundational characteristic of a lady. Kindness without intent or design was presented as one of the most valued features women possessed, or could posses. These points seem to suggest that there were certain traits of character and behaviour which it was thought beneficial for a lady to possess. Thus, to be a lady meant being modest, kind and caring.

However, there were also certain traits which were seen as undesirable. Traits which were not thought to be characteristic of a lady were snobbery and pretension. This meant imitating the way other people lived, and it meant deceiving others with false claims of status or income. Fakery, imitation and deceit were hardly the actions of someone secure in their position, and a lady was supposed to be secure in her position, wherever that led her to stand in the order of precedence. As well as being devoid of snobbery and pretension, a lady was not supposed to be self-important.

To illustrate this, we could imagine that there were two ladies living in a village. One was called Mrs C and the other Mrs D. Whilst Mrs C might have been the social equal of Mrs D – or perhaps even her superior – it is not hard to imagine that she would not be held in high esteem by her neighbours if she was snobbish, pretentious and self-important. In contrast, Mrs D was the very embodiment of kindness and consideration. Presumably, her circle of acquaintance would have therefore adored her.

In addition, there were other points of etiquette which were chiefly aimed at ladies. The first of these matters to be addressed here is how a lady was supposed to dress. Fashion is a fiendish friend, and what was in and out of fashion for ladies varied enormously over the course of the century. The high-waisted gowns which were popular in the early part of the century would have looked rather out of place in later decades, to take just one example. Nevertheless, there were some principles of etiquette with regard to dress – some points relating to conduct and taste – which ladies would have endeavoured to bear in mind. Or that was the case according to various etiquette manuals, at least. And at the end of the day, it is arbiters of etiquette who interest us here, not the arbiters of fashion.

To begin, a lady would have strived to cultivate an air of good taste and refinement in her dress. This would have meant ensuring that her dress was typified by elegant simplicity. A lady would also have been a follower of fashion, rather than a leader. Any sense of excess or affection in a lady's attire – such as undue ornamentation or the carrying of any particular fashion to an extreme – would have been assiduously avoided. As just discussed, it was not in the character of a lady to seek attention and admiration. In short, a lady's attire should have been unobtrusive and understated. If a lady's outfit was loud, fussy, daring or eccentric, it would seem that those guided by the demands of etiquette would have concluded that it was a bad one.

Furthermore, a lady would have sought to be neatly and properly dressed at all times, even when she was not expecting to see anyone. It was thought that a scrupulous approach to dress would have added to a lady's sense of propriety and dignity. It would have been wholly unacceptable for a lady to appear before company in untidy, unclean or slovenly clothing. Laxity in a lady's dress suggested laxity in her life and habits, and perhaps even in her mind and character. Personal cleanliness was also of the utmost importance. A lady would not have been negligent of her teeth, hair, nails and skin.

CHAPTER TEN

Let us imagine for a moment that a ballroom was filled with ladies and gentlemen dressed in their finest attire, which had been arranged with the highest degree of care and attention. And then let us suppose that the arrival of a young lady was announced. She entered with her hair in disarray, with the hem of her gown in dire need of an appointment with a needle and some thread, and with ink stains on her fingers from writing letters that morning. It is possible that the hostess might have felt slighted, perhaps feeling that the carelessness of the young lady's appearance suggested a lack of interest in the ball. It was a ball which our, admittedly imaginary, hostess would most likely have planned with diligence and meticulous care. If we place ourselves in the shoes of the hostess, she might well have thought that if she had gone to all of the trouble that came with throwing a ball, then it was not unreasonable of her to expect her guests to make some sort of attempt to look presentable.

Discernment and discretion also accompanied neatness and tidiness in the pursuit of good taste. A lady's dress was supposed to be flattering to her age and general appearance. There was, after all, no point in a lady following a fashion if it was not to her advantage. Consequently, a lady would have sought to dress in the colours and shades which suited her best. This was a matter of some discussion. In the first half of the century, *The Mirror of Graces* believed that white was a flattering colour for all young ladies. However, if they wanted to wear something more colourful, young ladies with a fuller figure were advised to choose bolder colours such as crimson and scarlet and richer shades of purple and yellow. It was said that ladies who were slightly built were more suited to paler shades of colours such as green, yellow, lilac and pink.

In the second half of the century, *Mixing in Society* proposed that paler colours should be worn by those with fair hair, whilst brunettes and those with dark hair were better suited to deeper, richer colours. However, age was also a factor in selecting colour. It was felt that elderly ladies with a slight figure should select paler colours. Black and dark grey were the recommended colours for older ladies with a fuller figure.

However, there were further considerations with regard to the colour of a lady's gown or attire. During the middle years of the century, *The Etiquette of Fashionable Life* warned ladies to avoid having clashing, glaring colours in their attire. Apparently, a want of judgment in this matter was suggestive of vulgarity and bad taste.

Additionally, a lady would have chosen the colour of a gown she intended to wear in the evening by candlelight.[3] By doing this, the lady would have been able to see the effect as it would appear in the evening, which might have been somewhat different to how the colour looked in daylight.

As well as selecting the right colour, there were other matters of taste that ladies were counselled to consider when putting together their outfits. These included taking such things as the pattern on a fabric or the style of an accessory into account. So for instance, if a lady was small, it was remarked that she would have been overwhelmed by her dress if it had a large pattern or heavy trimmings.[4] With regard to jewellery, *The Mirror of Graces* recommended that silver looked better on fair women, whilst brunettes appeared more advantageously wearing gold. Fair-haired ladies and brunettes both suited jewels such as pearls, diamonds and coral, whilst the former also suited stones such as emeralds, garnets and rubies.

However, as well as instructing ladies on how to dress tastefully, etiquette manuals also gave advice relating to bad taste. Dressing in bad taste was something a lady would naturally have been desirous to avoid. To begin on this subject, a lady would have dressed in a manner which was fitting for the time of year. An outfit which did not take into account the demands of the season, and which did not provide the required comfort or protection, was not an appropriate outfit. And, consequently, it was an outfit indicative of poor taste.

Equally, a lady's attire needed to be suitable for the occasion at hand. A lady would have appeared ridiculous if she embarked on a country walk in an outfit that was clearly only fit for travelling in a carriage, or indeed dancing in a ballroom. Whilst she might have looked very fine when she set out on her walk, it is likely that the effect would have been rather different by the time she returned home.

CHAPTER TEN

By the same token, a lady would have needed to take the time of day into consideration. A lady's clothes were supposed to be more simple and unobtrusive in the morning. Therefore, a lady was advised to limit the amount of jewellery she wore during the day. This included such times as when she was paying calls or receiving visitors. It was not until the evening that a lady was supposed to put on things that were expensive and shiny, for example for dinner. However, this is speaking on the matter in general terms. There was some interesting guidance on this subject, which brings us back to a point we have repeated quite a few times so far. Etiquette, and guidance on etiquette, differed over the course of the century.

Etiquette, Social Ethics and the Courtesies of Society felt that jewellery was best avoided in the morning, and should have been limited to a few gold trinkets if it was worn. Similarly, *The Book of Household Management* instructed ladies that jewellery should not form a part of their morning attire. *Mixing in Society* directed that jewellery worn during the morning should be confined to a brooch, a gold chain and a watch. Diamonds, pearls, rubies and other precious, transparent stones belonged to evening wear and were said to be wholly unsuitable for daytime attire. *Etiquette: What to Do and How to Do It* also advised ladies to restrict the amount of jewellery they wore in the morning, claiming that a brooch, a watch, earrings and perhaps a bracelet and a ring or two would have been quite sufficient. However, when considering whether to wear diamonds or pearls at this time of day, the advice given was that solitaire diamond earrings were permissible, but that all other diamonds were out of bounds. Pearls could be worn throughout the day, but that was because pearls needed to be worn during both night and day to preserve their colour.

Thus, broadly speaking, if we picture a lady paying her morning calls whilst dripping in diamonds or other precious stones, we could say that she was simply trying to bring a bit of sparkle to everyone's day. Alternatively, perhaps this was a lady unaware of etiquette guidance surrounding matters of dress. More critically, such an outfit might have looked as though the lady was trying to make some sort of point, or that she was trying just a bit too hard. In whatever way it was viewed, we can say that it was not in line with contemporary etiquette advice.

A further example of bad taste, which a lady was supposed to avoid, was the wearing of overly costly apparel. It was said that a lady managed to dress well by relying on her judgement, not by laying out large sums of money on expensive clothing and other accompanying items. The wife of a peer might have been able to avail herself of a new dress in very pricey fabric with perfect ease of mind, but the wife of a young gentleman just starting out in business could hardly have acted in the same way. A lady with a sense of propriety and judgement was supposed to be able to dress herself perfectly well, regardless of her income.

It would therefore seem that the etiquette of dress, as laid out in the etiquette manuals examined here, meant dressing in clothes which were suited to the lady in question and suitable for the occasion or hour when she was wearing them. This was also shaped by ideas of what constituted good taste, which seems to have been closely linked to discretion. In short, a lady was supposed to be neatly, tastefully and appropriately dressed at all times. Anything less was really just not on.

Another matter which often fell under a lady's care was the management of a household. This might also have meant that a lady had a husband. Briefly put, a happy husband – if there was one in situ – helped to make a happy home. In consequence, ladies were supposed to render themselves agreeable to their spouse. Wives were advised to continue to take care of their appearance, to greet their husband with a smile, and to generally endeavour to make the home comfortable and welcoming for him.

Nevertheless, there were some managerial and logistical concerns in relation to running a household which a lady would also have had to handle. In the same way that a lady was supposed to steer clear of extravagance in her spending on clothing, she would ideally have extended this prudence to the running of her establishment. It was said that a home was best maintained on the principles of good economy, which went hand in hand with the principles of good taste. Where luxurious furnishings were beyond the means of a lady, some judgement on her part meant that she could still render a room very pleasing. A clean, tidy home with well-placed furniture and an air of comfort could hardly have been considered objectionable by any sensible person. Flowers were recommended as a way of brightening a room without incurring any great expense.[5] As well as this, ladies were advised to keep their household accounts in strict order. Avoiding them would not make them go away.

Some Principal Points of Politeness

- There were certain qualities which it was said that a lady ought to possess.
- A lady was supposed to be modest, reserved, moral and kind.
- However, she was not supposed to be snobbish or pretentious.
- Nevertheless, a lady still had to look the part. A lady would have worn clothes which were suitable for the time of day and the occasion for which she was wearing them.
- One particular rule of etiquette was that a lady would have worn unobtrusive or few items of jewellery in the morning. She would have saved her diamonds for evening wear.
- She was also advised to select her clothes based on what suited her.
- Equally importantly, her clothes would have been clean and tidy.
- A lady might also have found herself running a household, and in this case, she would have kept her accounts regularly and with exacting accuracy.

CHAPTER ELEVEN

Particular Hints for Gentlemen

We could perhaps imagine that the perfect gentleman would have been possessed of a whole host of qualities and skills that set him apart from the merely average gentleman. Whilst an average gentleman would have been able to use his cutlery correctly, a perfect gentleman would have done so with aplomb. An average gentleman might have spoken with a lady politely, but a perfect gentleman would have been a delightful conversationalist. Naturally, the comparisons could go on. Of course, whether or not such a gentleman – one who was completely perfect in every possible and conceivable way – has ever existed, is perhaps a slightly debatable point. Differing conclusions are likely to arise.

Nevertheless, whilst perfection may or may not have been achieved, there were some points of etiquette which were particularly directed towards gentlemen. These points of etiquette related to the behaviours and habits which gentlemen in the nineteenth century were advised by etiquette manuals to adopt. Over the course of the following pages, we shall look at the practice of smoking, the etiquette of dress and the hints which were given to husbands. However, as discussed in the preceding chapter, the question of personal qualities was an important one. And, just as it was raised with ladies, it was also raised with gentlemen. Thus, we shall explore what it meant to be a gentleman, and which qualities were considered to be especially gentlemanly.

Towards the beginning of the century, *Principles of Politeness* detailed the importance of modesty for gentlemen. A gentleman would not have boasted about his marvellous abilities, large estate, grand circle of acquaintance, or indeed about any other matter at all. For example, it is not difficult to imagine that having a boastful gentleman as a dinner companion, whose only subject of conversation was his high opinion of himself, would have been a rather trying experience.

However, although a gentleman would have been modest, he would not have been shy or awkward. A gentleman would have been self-assured, regardless of the company in which he was mixing. He would have found confidence in the knowledge that he was a gentleman. Regardless of how rich, grand or important one gentleman might have been in comparison with another, both of them were still gentlemen at the end of the day.[1]

A gentleman would also have been able to adapt his manner to the company in which he found himself. Towards his superiors, he would have been respectful. Amongst his equals and inferiors, he would have been open and at his ease. However, he would never have been so at his ease as to allow himself to cross the line into improper or discourteous conduct. In short, according to this line of advice, a gentleman's character would ideally have been a mixture of confidence and modesty. These both would also have been accompanied by the sort of sound judgement which would have enabled him to mix and mingle politely in society.

Accordingly, we shall take the examples of the hypothetical Mr A and the hypothetical Mr B. Both gentlemen were equals in rank, fortune and education. They mixed in the same circles. However, Mr A avoided speaking of his own achievements. If he ever was obliged to speak of them in some way, his did so with modesty. He was respectful towards his superiors, but did not stand in awe of them. He was respectful in his conduct and address amongst his equals and inferiors as well. In contrast, Mr B had acquired an unfortunate habit of only talking about himself. And this habit was sadly accompanied by what can only be described as an air of arrogance. Or at least, this was the case amongst his equals and inferiors. When in the company of his superiors, he most regrettably seemed to replace his arrogance with awkwardness. So, if we follow the advice which was given in etiquette manuals, it would appear that Mr A had a more gentlemanly character, or at least displayed more gentlemanly qualities, than Mr B. It is hard not to feel a little sorry for Mr B, actually.

There were further qualities and marks of gentlemanly character which etiquette manuals felt their readers ought to possess. For instance, it was felt that a gentleman would have been considerate and kind-hearted.[2] This would have been particularly apparent in his conduct towards women, children and the poor.[3] So, if we take this trait and consider what it might have meant for behaviour, we could perhaps imagine that a gentleman would not have angrily pushed his way past a man or woman who walked slower than him on the street. Or, we could say that a gentleman would not have used coarse language and vulgar expressions in the presence of women and children.[4] As well as the above, we could assume that a gentleman would not have been contemptuous and arrogant towards those less fortunately situated in life.

An additional mark of a gentleman would have been his scrupulous honesty and truthfulness. If a gentleman was in the wrong, or had committed a fault, he would not have hesitated to own up to it and apologise for it. He would never have knowingly engaged in any sort of deceit. A gentleman's honour and good name were of the utmost importance.

Another matter to consider is the character traits and conduct which gentlemen were cautioned to avoid. It was said that a gentleman would always have avoided forwardness and over-familiarity. He would have maintained an appropriate amount of civil and respectful reserve at all times. For example, imagine how it would have looked if one gentleman was introduced to another, and then the former instantly began to behave towards the latter as though they had been intimate acquaintances for the previous decade or two. It might well have looked presumptuous, amongst other things.

In brief and as previously discussed with regard to ladies, we must take the distinction between internal feelings and outward behaviour into account, and understand that there is a difference between them. Yet, it was nevertheless felt that a gentleman would have been, or at least ought to have been, possessed of a multitude of commendable qualities. These qualities were discussed over the course of the century. And whilst we can safely say that it would certainly have been advantageous for a gentleman to be rich, we could perhaps also say that when it came to having a gentlemanly character, there was a currency of conduct which counted just as much as the type of currency a bank clerk would have recorded in his ledger. One etiquette manual from the early part of the century remarked that the marks of a gentleman would have shone through, even if he had been reduced to rags.[5]

Though quite understandably, it certainly would have helped a gentleman if he was attired in something rather more suitable and substantial than rags. It was an important point of etiquette for a gentleman to be appropriately dressed. Of course, fashion has never exactly been a loyal friend to its followers, and gentlemen's fashion underwent a significant change around the early part of the century. The flamboyant attire of the eighteenth century shifted towards a simpler style of clothing. With Beau Brummell leading the way, a more moderate palette replaced the bright colours previously favoured. Under his direction, the principal components of a well-dressed gentleman's outfit would have included a dark coat, a light waistcoat and an impeccably tied cravat. Gentlemen's fashion became increasingly focussed on the precision of the cut, the quality of the cloth and the overall style. Of course, fashion had its moments, and different occasions called for different outfits, but Brummell's decrees on what constituted good taste continued to influence gentlemen's fashion throughout the rest of the century.

With reference to the etiquette of selecting appropriate attire, gentlemen were exhorted not to try and be leaders of fashion. There was not supposed to be anything eccentric or extreme in their clothing. Similarly, a gentleman would have been restrained in his use of personal ornamentation. After all, a gentleman was a gentleman, not a magpie hankering after shiny trinkets. For example, advice given in the second half of the century told gentlemen to limit their jewellery to such items as a set of studs, a watch and perhaps a ring or two.[6]

Additionally, a gentleman would have been neat and careful with his attire. It would not have been fitting for a gentleman to venture out with a mark on his coat or a scuff on his shoes. For instance, as the 1840s drew to a close, *The Etiquette of Fashionable Life* decreed that it was very poor form for a gentleman to don an un-brushed coat. Etiquette manuals also reiterated the value of a good fit and quality tailoring. The importance of tidiness extended to personal hygiene. Gentlemen were instructed to keep their hair, teeth and nails clean. Needless to say, a gentleman would not have willingly or knowingly inflicted an unpleasant odour on others.

As mentioned briefly, different occasions required different clothing. Thus, as we have discussed before, a frock coat was suitable for the daily bustle of the street, but a dress coat was needed for evenings in the drawing room. Other matters of clothing etiquette included the expectation that a gentleman would wear gloves when out on the street, in a church or at the theatre. It was also said that, when out and about, a gentleman would have carried an umbrella or stick with him.[7]

Let us picture again two imaginary gentlemen by the names of Mr C and Mr D. Both were attending the theatre one night. Mr C had forgotten to brush both his coat and his hair. He had also forgotten his gloves. Mr D, on the contrary, was correctly and impeccably turned out. With regard to success in adhering to the etiquette of gentlemanly dress, it would seem safe to conclude that Mr D would have won.

To be concise, according to the etiquette advice given during this period, the best-dressed gentleman would have been the one whose clothing generated no comment. He would have dressed in a manner befitting the occasion at hand and the time of day. He would not have worn garish colours or daring fashions, and his clothing and person would both have been clean.

Two further matters of etiquette which were particularly pertinent for gentlemen were the taking of snuff and smoking. As with clothing, this once again means that our exploration of etiquette can also include some of the physical objects which made up the nineteenth-century world. These lend depth to our attempt to imagine the lives and experiences of ladies and gentlemen – or more particularly in this instance, of gentlemen – during this period.

CHAPTER ELEVEN

In the earlier part of the century, the taking of snuff was more prevalent than smoking. Indeed, there was a particular art and grace to the taking of snuff, and gentlemen would have endeavoured to open their snuff boxes with the requisite flair. Written towards the beginning of the century, *Principles of Politeness* advised gentlemen that they should conduct themselves with ease when they were in the company of their equals. This notion of ease included the belief that a gentleman should feel free to take snuff. Taking snuff was perfectly appropriate in those circumstances. However, it must be said that it would have been quite unacceptable for a gentleman to have whistled or loosened his garters. Of course, it should be stressed that taking snuff was not a pastime which was exclusive to gentlemen. Queen Charlotte – the wife of George III – was a particularly avid taker of snuff, for instance.

Although smoking was initially less common at the start of the century and often frowned upon, it became increasingly popular. Broadly speaking, it was thought best that gentlemen did not smoke in the presence of ladies. Gentlemen were also strongly advised against smoking in the street or, more generally, in any place where the practice might have proved to be a nuisance to others.

The next issue to which we shall turn our attention concerns money and income. Gentlemen were exhorted to live within their means. *A System of Etiquette* from the first half of the century went into some detail on this matter. Thus, one rather sound piece of advice which was given was that a gentleman should not buy something unless he had the ability to pay for it. A gentleman's management of his income was also discussed. If a gentleman lived off the income from his estate, he was counselled to work out what that income was, and then plan his expenses so that they fell beneath that amount. After all, if a gentleman's estate brought him £3,000 a year, this did not really help him if he lived as though he had £5,000 a year. Gentlemen who drew their income from a sum of capital were advised to live only upon the interest this capital gave them. At the end of the day, if a gentleman began reducing the capital, his interest would have reduced in turn, and then he might one day have found that he was living in noticeably reduced circumstances.

Gentlemen who had been so fortunate as to have secured the blessing of a wife were advised to allot a certain amount for the running of the house and to give this to their wife at the appointed time, be that weekly, monthly or quarterly.[8] Once the money had been handed over, they were counselled to allow their wife to run her domain as she saw fit. Husbands were supposed to interfere as little as possible. In short, and perhaps in rather unfittingly modern terms, gentlemen were advised not to micro-manage the household expenditure of their wives.

Husbands were also advised to be open with their wives about money and the household budget.[9] So for example, if a husband needed his wife to be more economical than before – perhaps if they were faced with increased financial pressure – then it would have been sensible for the husband to tell the wife frankly and plainly. It would have been deeply unfair for a husband to be cross with his wife for running their household as she had done for however many years previously, without introducing any new economies, if he had not told her that they needed to be made. However many skills that hypothetical gentleman's wife may have had, it is highly unlikely that they included the ability to read people's minds.

Moving away from the rather taxing issue of finances, there were some additional points of politeness which it was recommended that gentlemen should adopt with reference to their wives. Gentlemen were supposed to be solicitous of their wives' wants and needs, to keep them in a comfortable situation and to treat them with kindness. A wife had entrusted her future happiness to her husband, and this was a responsibility he was expected to take seriously. A husband was also supposed to cultivate a high opinion of his wife. And, if a gentleman's wife was not an ideal wife, if she was cross towards him or negligent towards their home, then the gentleman was advised to consider if he was perhaps the cause of her negative attitude.

Some Principal Points of Politeness

- A gentleman was supposed to be kind, modest and truthful.
- He was expected to be respectful towards his superiors, but remain at his ease.
- In the company of his equals and inferiors, he would never have allowed his sense of ease to induce him to behave in an improper fashion.
- A gentleman would have dressed neatly and tidily.
- He would also have paid attention to his personal hygiene.
- He would have remembered to wear the correct clothes at the correct time. For example, he would have worn gloves to the theatre.
- A gentleman would not have dressed in unusual or eccentric clothing.
- He would also have managed his money properly.
- He would have endeavoured to be a good husband to his wife as well.

A Concluding Comment

The problem with conclusions is that grand, sweeping statements tend not to work very well. Whilst they might sound nice, there will generally be at least a few exceptions to every rule. Therefore, we have to be careful about how we look at – and think about – the past. When it comes to the behaviour of ladies and gentlemen in the nineteenth century, we have to take into account that people were simply people. They had their own views and beliefs, their own habits and customs, and their own follies and foibles. For example, a quick glance at a novel by Jane Austen will make it clear that whilst a man or woman might have been considered a lady or gentleman by society, that status did not stop them from being rude or ridiculous.

Thus, whilst we can look at the etiquette which was advocated over the course of the century, we cannot conclude that this meant that everyone, at all times, behaved according to those recommendations. After all, we have seen how etiquette guidance changed over the course of the century. The proper way to eat a piece of fish would be a good piece of evidence to submit in order to underline this point. And, with that point, it is important to bear in mind that there would have been different generations living side by side. Not only that, but it is hard not to imagine that some individuals would have had their own individual preferences. As well as this, there would have been some ladies and gentlemen used to a very opulent style of living, whilst others would have had to get by with far fewer luxuries. For example, a respectable spinster living in a small cottage with a limited income could have been a lady, just like the one in the manor house. However, her circumstances would have meant that she lived a rather different life.

In addition, it seems sensible that we ought to consider our nineteenth-century forebears as human beings prone to human flaws.

A CONCLUDING COMMENT

It is hard to picture the nineteenth century as a world inhabited by ladies and gentlemen who did not have bad days, or days when they were worried, or days when they were cross, or days when they were forgetful, or days when they simply made an error of judgement. Perhaps it should be whispered quietly, but ladies and gentlemen might have even had days when they simply got out of the wrong side of the bed. In short, there might have been many causes for people to have behaved differently to one another. And, by extension, there are many reasons why the recommendations put forward in etiquette manuals might not have been followed. Or at least, many reasons why they might not always have been followed all of the time.

Nevertheless, the etiquette advice detailed in manuals over the course of the nineteenth century allows us to consider what was thought to be polite. Exploring etiquette enables us – or indeed, has enabled us – to consider the customs and habits which would have formed part of the lives of ladies and gentlemen.

Our exploration of etiquette has covered a variety of polite practices, ranging from everyday habits such as taking a walk or paying calls, to what we could consider the highlights of people's social calendars, such as balls and dinner parties. We have been able to uncover and imagine numerous aspects of nineteenth-century life and nineteenth-century experiences. Amongst other things, we have looked at where ladies and gentlemen might have sat in a carriage, how they might have gone into dinner, how they might have spoken to and addressed other people, how they might have behaved when walking down a street, and many other points of etiquette from this period. These points of etiquette are all expressions of social conventions. They have helped us to create some sort of picture as to what daily life might have been like for normal, everyday people. Or at any rate, for normal, everyday people who were at least reasonably well off.

As well as this, there were many trappings that went along with following etiquette – having the right clothes, having cards to leave for acquaintances and so on – which the etiquette manuals naturally detailed. Whilst it might sound dismissive to refer to them as the 'trappings' of etiquette, they are certainly not something to be dismissed out of hand. Having the right clothes and having cards to leave were necessary for ladies and gentlemen, as they enabled them to participate in the civilities which etiquette manuals discussed. Looking at what made a good outfit or a correct card also provides us with an insight into the things ladies and gentlemen would have touched and handled during this period. Similarly, other objects have featured time and time again through the course of this book, in the form of ink, paper, sealing wax, wafers, jewellery, dance cards, carriages, hats, umbrellas and more. These were normal sights and everyday objects for ladies and gentlemen in the nineteenth century. Well, the luxuries of diamonds, pearls and private carriages might perhaps have been sights of some note in certain instances. Regardless, this physical element underlines that for us these 'trappings' are pieces of history. They are all significant because they highlight details of daily life, the patterns which daily life followed and are consequently interesting in their own right.

So, whilst we cannot make a grand conclusion, we could perhaps attempt to make a more modest one. We have been able to use etiquette guidance to explore both the practices of politeness and the physical objects which went along with those practices. In so doing, we have added detail to our understanding of the lives and experiences of ladies and gentlemen during this period. We have also tried to bring something of the nineteenth-century world back to life and imagine the people, places and objects which made up that world. And, although we have not quite managed to travel back in time, it could nevertheless be said that the attempt has met with at least some small measure of success.

Notes

Chapter 1

1. Lady Constance Howard, *Etiquette: What to Do and How to Do It* (London: F.V. White and Co., 1885), p. 140.
2. Ibid.
3. Anon., *Manners and Rules of Good Society, Or Solecisms to be Avoided*, 20th edn (London and New York: Frederick Warne and Co., 1894), p. 55.
4. Howard, *Etiquette: What to Do and How to Do It*, p. 391.
5. Ibid.
6. Anon., *Etiquette, Social Ethics and the Courtesies of Society* (London: Wm. S. Orr and Co., 1854), p. 63.
7. Anon., *Mixing in Society: A Complete Manual of Manners* (London and New York: George Routledge and Sons, 1870), p. 248.

Chapter Two

1. James Ansell, *Principles of Politeness, And of Knowing the World*, Parts I and II, (Antwerp: A. Allebé, 1804), Part II, p. 8.
2. Anon., *Hints on Etiquette and the Usages of Society: With a Glance at Bad Habits*, 2nd edn (London: Longman, Rees, Orme, Brown, Green and Longman, 1836), p. 15.
3. Anon., *Etiquette for Gentlemen: With Hints on the Art of Conversation* (London: Charles Tilt, 1838), p. 16.
4. Lady Constance Howard, *Etiquette: What to Do and How to Do It* (London: F.V. White and Co., 1885), p. 142. Anon., *Manners and Rules of Good Society, Or Solecisms to be Avoided*, 20th edn (London and New York: Frederick Warne and Co., 1894), p. 7.
5. Howard, *Etiquette: What to Do and How to Do It*, p. 143. Anon., *Manners and Rules of Good Society*, p. 9.
6. Ibid., p. 11.

7. Arthur Freeling, *The Pocket Book of Etiquette* (Liverpool: Henry Lacey, 1837), p. 9.

8. The Revd Dr John Trusler, *A System of Etiquette*, 2nd edn (Bath: M. Gye, *c.* 1804[?]), p. 15.

9. Anon., *Hints on Etiquette and the Usages of Society*, p. 17.

10. Anon., *Mixing in Society: A Complete Manual of Manners* (London and New York: George Routledge and Sons, 1870), p. 77.

11. Anon., *Etiquette, Social Ethics and the Courtesies of Society* (London: Wm. S. Orr and Co., 1854), p. 44.

Chapter Three

1. Lady Constance Howard, *Etiquette: What to Do and How to Do It* (London: F.V. White and Co., 1885), p. 348.

2. Mrs Humphrey, *Manners for Men* (Exeter: Webb and Bower Ltd, 1979; first published 1897), p. 137.

3. Howard, *Etiquette: What to Do and How to Do It*, p. 339.

4. Ibid., p. 340. Anon., *Manners and Rules of Good Society, Or Solecisms to be Avoided*, 20th edn (London and New York: Frederick Warne and Co., 1894), p. 181.

5. Howard, *Etiquette: What to Do and How to Do It*, p. 340.

6. Humphrey, *Manners for Men*, p. 19.

7. Anon., *Manners and Rules of Good Society*, p. 183. Humphrey, *Manners for Men*, p. 13.

8. Anon., *All About Etiquette; Or, the Manners of Polite Society: For Ladies, Gentlemen and Families* (London: Ward, Lock & Co., 1875[?]), p. 176.

9. Anon., *Etiquette for All, Or Rules of Conduct for Every Circumstance in Life: with the Laws, Rules, Precepts and Practices of Good Society* (Glasgow: George Watson, 1861), p. 45.

10. Ibid.

11. Anon., *All About Etiquette*, p. 175.

12. Howard, *Etiquette: What to Do and How to Do It*, pp. 348–9.

13. Anon., *Manners and Rules of Good Society*, p. 185.

14. Howard, *Etiquette: What to Do and How to Do It*, p. 349.

15. Anon., *Manners and Rules of Good Society*, p. 186.

16. Howard, *Etiquette: What to Do and How to Do It*, p. 350.

17. Ibid., p. 139.

18. Ibid., p. 349.

19. Ibid., p. 140.

20. Ibid., p. 349. Anon., *Manners and Rules of Good Society*, pp. 185–6.

21. Anon., *Manners and Rules of Good Society*, p. 186.

22. Anon., *Mixing in Society: A Complete Manual of Manners* (London and New York: George Routledge and Sons, 1870), p. 137.

23. Howard, *Etiquette: What to Do and How to Do It*, p. 349.

24. Ibid. Anon., *Manners and Rules of Good Society*, p. 186.

Chapter Four

1. Lady Constance Howard, *Etiquette: What to Do and How to Do It* (London: F.V. White and Co., 1885), p. 183.

2. Ibid.

3. Ibid.

4. Ibid., p. 184.

5. Mrs Humphrey, *Manners for Men* (Exeter: Webb and Bower Ltd, 1979; first published 1897), p. 121.

6. Howard, *Etiquette: What to Do and How to Do It*, p. 184.

7. Ibid.

8. Ibid., p. 190.

9. Anon., *Mixing in Society: A Complete Manual of Manners* (London and New York: George Routledge and Sons, 1870), p. 82.

10. The Revd Dr John Trusler, *A System of Etiquette*, 2nd edn (Bath: M. Gye, *c.* 1804[?]), p. 30.

11. Anon., *Hints on Etiquette and the Usages of Society: With a Glance at Bad Habits*, 2nd edn (London: Longman, Rees, Orme, Brown, Green and Longman, 1836), p. 54.

12. Arthur Freeling, *The Pocket Book of Etiquette* (Liverpool: Henry Lacey, 1837), p. 22. Anon., *The Ladies' Pocket Book of Etiquette*, 7th edn (London and Liverpool: George Bell and H. Lacey, 1840), p. 32.

13. Anon., *Mixing in Society*, p. 81.

14. Anon., *All About Etiquette; Or, the Manners of Polite Society:*

For Ladies, Gentlemen and Families (London: Ward, Lock & Co., 1875[?]), p. 196.

15. Howard, *Etiquette: What to Do and How to Do It*, p. 211.

16. Anon., *Manners and Rules of Good Society, Or Solecisms to be Avoided*, 20th edn (London and New York: Frederick Warne and Co., 1894), p. 29. Humphrey, *Manners for Men*, p. 122.

17. Howard, *Etiquette: What to Do and How to Do It*, p. 197. Anon., *Manners and Rules of Good Society*, p. 18.

18. Howard, *Etiquette: What to Do and How to Do It*, p. 200. Anon., *Manners and Rules of Good Society*, p. 19.

19. Howard, *Etiquette: What to Do and How to Do It*, p. 222. Anon., *Manners and Rules of Good Society*, p. 31.

20. Humphrey, *Manners for Men*, p. 122.

21. Freeling, *The Pocket Book of Etiquette*, p. 22. Anon., *The Ladies' Pocket Book of Etiquette*, pp. 31–2.

22. Anon., *Etiquette, Social Ethics and the Courtesies of Society* (London: Wm. S. Orr and Co., 1854), p. 20.

23. Isabella Beeton, *The Book of Household Management* (London: S.O. Beeton, 1861), p. 10.

24. Anon., *Mixing in Society*, p. 82. Anon., *All About Etiquette*, p. 195.

25. Anon., *Manners and Rules of Good Society*, p. 33.

26. Humphrey, *Manners for Men*, p. 127.

Chapter Five

1. Anon., *The Ladies' Pocket Book of Etiquette*, 7th edn (London and Liverpool: George Bell and H. Lacey, 1840), p. 48.

2. Anon., *Etiquette for All, Or Rules of Conduct for Every Circumstance in Life: with the Laws, Rules, Precepts and Practices of Good Society* (Glasgow: George Watson, 1861), p. 25.

3. Lady Constance Howard, *Etiquette: What to Do and How to Do It* (London: F.V. White and Co., 1885), p. 4. Anon., *Manners and Rules of Good Society, Or Solecisms to be Avoided*, 20th edn (London and New York: Frederick Warne and Co., 1894), p. 97.

4. Anon., *Manners and Rules of Good Society*, p. 96. Mrs Humphrey, *Manners for Men* (Exeter: Webb and Bower Ltd, 1979; first published 1897), p. 55.

5. The Revd Dr John Trusler, *A System of Etiquette*, 2nd edn (Bath: M. Gye, *c.* 1804[?]), p. 37.

6. Howard, *Etiquette: What to Do and How to Do It*, p. 8. Anon., *Manners and Rules of Good Society*, p. 97.

7. Howard, *Etiquette: What to Do and How to Do It*, p. 8.

8. Anon., *Etiquette for Gentlemen: With Hints on the Art of Conversation* (London: Charles Tilt, 1838), p. 28.

9. Anon., *Mixing in Society: A Complete Manual of Manners* (London and New York: George Routledge and Sons, 1870), pp. 175–6.

10. Anon., *Etiquette, Social Ethics and the Courtesies of Society* (London: Wm. S. Orr and Co., 1854), p. 22.

11. Howard, *Etiquette: What to Do and How to Do It*, p. 309. Anon., *Manners and Rules of Good Society*, p. 46.

12. Trusler, *A System of Etiquette*, p. 40.

13. Anon., *Hints on Etiquette and the Usages of Society: With a Glance at Bad Habits*, 2nd edn (London: Longman, Rees, Orme, Brown, Green and Longman, 1836), p. 24. Anon., *Etiquette, Social Ethics and the Courtesies of Society*, p. 13.

14. Anon., *Etiquette, Social Ethics and the Courtesies of Society*, p. 12.

15. Anon., *Manners and Rules of Good Society*, p. 102.

16. Anon., *Etiquette for Gentlemen*, p. 29.

17. Howard, *Etiquette: What to Do and How to Do It*, p. 34.

18. Anon., *Manners and Rules of Good Society*, p. 105.

19. Anon., *Mixing in Society*, p. 197. Howard, *Etiquette: What to Do and How to Do It*, p. 47.

20. Anon., *Mixing in Society*, p. 197.

21. Ibid.

22. Ibid. Howard, *Etiquette: What to Do and How to Do It*, p. 47.

23. Anon., *Hints on Etiquette and the Usages of Society*, p. 28.

24. Anon., *Manners and Rules of Good Society*, p. 106.

25. Ibid.

26. Anon., *Mixing in Society*, p. 184.

27. Ibid., p. 186. Anon., *Manners and Rules of Good Society*, p. 118.

28. Anon., *The Ladies' Pocket Book of Etiquette*, p. 47.

29. Anon., *Etiquette for All*, p. 28.

30. Howard, *Etiquette: What to Do and How to Do It*, p. 52.

31. Humphrey, *Manners for Men*, p. 80.

32. Anon., *Hints on Etiquette and the Usages of Society*, p. 33.

Chapter Six

1. Mrs Humphrey, *Manners for Men* (Exeter: Webb and Bower Ltd, 1979; first published 1897), p. 104.

2. Anon., *Hints on Etiquette and the Usages of Society: With a Glance at Bad Habits*, 2nd edn (London: Longman, Rees, Orme, Brown, Green and Longman, 1836), p. 46. Anon., *All About Etiquette; Or, the Manners of Polite Society: For Ladies, Gentlemen and Families* (London: Ward, Lock & Co., 1875[?]), p. 108.

3. Jame Ansell, *Principles of Politeness, And of Knowing the World*, Parts I and II (Antwerp: A. Allebé, 1804), Part II, p. 10.

4. Anon., *Hints on Etiquette and the Usages of Society*, pp. 46–7. Anon., *All About Etiquette*, p. 107.

5. Anon., *Etiquette, Social Ethics and the Courtesies of Society* (London: Wm. S. Orr and Co., 1854), p. 17.

6. Anon., *Mixing in Society: A Complete Manual of Manners* (London and New York: George Routledge and Sons, 1870), p. 162.

7. Anon., *Etiquette, Social Ethics and the Courtesies of Society*, p. 16.

8. Anon., *Manners and Rules of Good Society, Or Solecisms to be Avoided*, 20th edn (London and New York: Frederick Warne and Co., 1894), p. 88.

9. W.H. Woakes, *An Essay on the Attitudes Derived from Gesture to be Attended to in Dancing, With Observations on the Art: Also, the Etiquette of the English Ball Room* (Hereford: W.H. and J. Parker, 1825[?]), p. 37.

10. Anon., *Mixing in Society*, p. 166.

11. Alfred E. Douglas, *The Etiquette of Fashionable Life: Including the Ball Room and the Court Etiquette of the Present Day* (London and Easingwold: Simpkin, Marshall, & Co., and Thomas Gill, 1849), p. 17.

Chapter Seven

1. Anon., *Mixing in Society: A Complete Manual of Manners* (London and New York: George Routledge and Sons, 1870), p. 102. Lady Constance Howard, *Etiquette: What to Do and How to Do It* (London: F.V. White and Co., 1885), p. 373.

Chapter Eight

1. Arthur Freeling, *The Pocket Book of Etiquette* (Liverpool: Henry Lacey, 1837), p. 58.
2. Anon., *The Ladies' Pocket Book of Etiquette*, 7th edn (London and Liverpool: George Bell and H. Lacey, 1840), p. 85.
3. Anon., *Mixing in Society: A Complete Manual of Manners* (London and New York: George Routledge and Sons, 1870), p. 60.
4. Mrs Sarah Stickney Ellis, *The Women Of England, Their Social Duties and Domestic Habits* (London: Fisher, Son and Co., 1839[?]), pp. 179–80.

Chapter Nine

1. Anon., *Etiquette, Social Ethics and the Courtesies of Society* (London: Wm. S. Orr and Co., 1854), p. 29.
2. Ibid.
3. Anon., *The Etiquette of Love, Courtship and Marriage, To which is Added the Etiquette of Politeness* (Halifax: Milner and Sowerby, 1859), p. 73.
4. Mrs Humphrey, *Manners for Men* (Exeter: Webb and Bower Ltd, 1979; first published 1897), p. 108.
5. Ibid.
6. Ibid.
7. Anon., *Mixing in Society: A Complete Manual of Manners* (London and New York: George Routledge and Sons, 1870), p. 220.
8. Anon., *Manners and Rules of Good Society, Or Solecisms to be Avoided*, 20th edn (London and New York: Frederick Warne and Co., 1894), p. 130.
9. Madame de Chatelain, *Bridal Etiquette* (London: Ward and Lock, 1856), p. 13.

10. Ibid.

11. Anon., *Manners and Rules of Good Society*, p. 130.

12. De Chatelain, *Bridal Etiquette*, p. 14.

13. Lady Constance Howard, *Etiquette: What to Do and How to Do It* (London: F.V. White and Co., 1885), p. 280. Anon., *Manners and Rules of Good Society*, p. 130.

14. Howard, *Etiquette: What to Do and How to Do It*, p. 277. Anon., *Manners and Rules of Good Society*, p. 123.

15. Anon., *Etiquette, Social Ethics and the Courtesies of Society*, p. 32.

16. Ibid.

17. Howard, *Etiquette: What to Do and How to Do It*, p. 306. Anon., *Manners and Rules of Good Society*, p. 132.

18. Howard, *Etiquette: What to Do and How to Do It*, p. 307.

19. Anon., *Manners and Rules of Good Society*, p. 133.

20. Ibid., p. 137.

21. Ibid.

22. Anon., *The Etiquette of Love, Courtship and Marriage*, p. 110.

23. Ibid.

24. Ibid., p. 109.

25. Howard, *Etiquette: What to Do and How to Do It*, p. 309. Anon., *Manners and Rules of Good Society*, p. 134.

26. Anon., *Hints on Etiquette and the Usages of Society: With a Glance at Bad Habits*, 2nd edn (London: Longman, Rees, Orme, Brown, Green and Longman, 1836), p. 19.

27. Anon., *The Ladies' Pocket Book of Etiquette*, 7th edn (London and Liverpool: George Bell and H. Lacey, 1840), p. 81.

28. De Chatelain, *Bridal Etiquette*, p. 18.

29. Howard, *Etiquette: What to Do and How to Do It*, p. 279. Anon., *Manners and Rules of Good Society*, p. 135.

30. Anon., *Manners and Rules of Good Society*, p. 135.

Chapter Ten

1. James Ansell, *Principles of Politeness, And of Knowing the World*, Parts I and II (Antwerp: A. Allebé, 1804), Part II, p. 3.

2. Anon., *The Ladies' Pocket Book of Etiquette*, 7th edn (London and Liverpool: George Bell and H. Lacey, 1840), p. 38.

3. Anon., *Mirror of Graces; Or, the English Lady's Costume* (London: B. Crosby and Co., 1811), p. 123.

4. Anon., *Etiquette for All, Or Rules of Conduct for Every Circumstance in Life: with the Laws, Rules, Precepts and Practices of Good Society* (Glasgow: George Watson, 1861), p. 42.

5. Anon., *Mixing in Society: A Complete Manual of Manners* (London and New York: George Routledge and Sons, 1870), p. 58.

Chapter Eleven

1. The Revd Dr John Trusler, *A System of Etiquette*, 2nd edn (Bath: M. Gye, *c.* 1804[?]), p. 5.

2. Mrs Humphrey, *Manners for Men* (Exeter: Webb and Bower Ltd, 1979; first published 1897), p. 2.

3. Ibid.

4. Ibid., p. 5.

5. The Revd Dr Trusler, *A Warm Appeal Against the Disturbers of Their Own Quiet, And that of Others* (Bath: H. Gye, 1816), p. 1.

6. Anon., *Mixing in Society: A Complete Manual of Manners* (London and New York: George Routledge and Sons, 1870), p. 128. Lady Constance Howard, *Etiquette: What to Do and How to Do It* (London: F.V. White and Co., 1885), p. 165.

7. Howard, *Etiquette: What to Do and How to Do It*, p. 166.

8. Anon., *Etiquette, Social Ethics and the Courtesies of Society* (London: Wm. S. Orr and Co., 1854), p. 40.

9. Ibid.

Bibliography

Etiquette Manuals

Anon., *All About Etiquette; Or, The Manners of Polite Society: For Ladies, Gentlemen and Families*, London: Ward, Lock, and Co., 1875[?]

Anon., *Etiquette for All, Or Rules of Conduct for Every Circumstance in Life: with the Laws, Rules, Precepts and Practices of Good Society*, Glasgow: George Watson, 1861

Anon., *Etiquette for Gentlemen: With Hints on the Art of Conversation*, London: Charles Tilt, 1838

Anon., *Etiquette, Social Ethics and the Courtesies of Society*, London: Wm. S. Orr & Co., 1854

Anon., *Hints on Etiquette and the Usages of Society: With a Glance at Bad Habits*, 2nd edn, London: Longman, Rees, Orme, Brown, Green and Longman, 1836

Anon., *Manners and Rules of Good Society, Or Solecisms to be Avoided*, 20th edn, London and New York: Frederick Warne and Co., 1894

Anon., *Mirror of Graces; Or, the English Lady's Costume*, London: B. Crosby and Co., 1811

Anon., *Mixing in Society: A Complete Manual of Manners*, London and New York: George Routledge and Sons, 1870

Anon., *The Etiquette of Love, Courtship and Marriage, To which is Added the Etiquette of Politeness*, Halifax: Milner and Sowerby, 1859

Anon., *The Ladies' Pocket Book of Etiquette*, 7th edn, London and Liverpool: George Bell, and H. Lacey, 1840

Ansell, James, *Principles of Politeness, And of Knowing the World*, Parts I and II, Antwerp: A. Allebé, 1804

Beeton, Isabella, *The Book of Household Management*, London: S.O. Beeton, 1861

BIBLIOGRAPHY

Burke, John, *A General and Heraldic Dictionary of the Peerage and Baronetage of the British Empire*, Vol. 1, 4th edn, London: Henry Colburn, 1833

Burke, John, *A General and Heraldic Dictionary of the Peerage and Baronetage of the British Empire*, Vol. 2, 4th edn, London: Henry Colburn, 1833

Butcher, John, *Instructions in Etiquette, For the Use of All; Five Letters on Important Subjects, Exclusively for Ladies; And Conversational Hints to whom Concerned*, 3rd edn, London and Nottingham: Simpkin, Marshall, and Co., and Dearden, 1847

Chatelain, Madame de, *Bridal Etiquette*, London: Ward and Lock, 1856

Douglas, Alfred E., *The Etiquette of Fashionable Life: Including the Ball Room and the Court Etiquette of the Present Day*, London and Easingwold: Simpkin, Marshall, & Co., and Thomas Gill, 1849

Ellis, Mrs Sarah Stickney, *The Women Of England, Their Social Duties and Domestic Habits*, London: Fisher, Son and Co., 1839[?]

Freeling, Arthur, *The Pocket Book of Etiquette*, Liverpool: Henry Lacey, 1837

Howard, Lady Constance, *Etiquette: What to Do and How to Do It*, London: F.V. White and Co., 1885

Humphrey, Mrs, *Manners for Men*, Exeter: Webb and Bower Ltd, 1979; first published 1897

Trusler, the Revd Dr John, *A System of Etiquette*, 2nd edn, Bath: M. Gye, *c.* 1804[?]

Trusler, the Revd Dr, *A Warm Appeal Against the Disturbers of their Own Quiet, And that of Others*, Bath: H. Gye, 1816

Woakes, W.H., *An Essay on the Attitudes Derived from Gesture to be Attended to in Dancing, With Observations on the Art: Also, the Etiquette of the English Ball Room*, Hereford: W.H. and J. Parker, 1825[?]

Additional Resources

Brooke, Christopher, *Jane Austen: Illusion and Reality*, Cambridge: D.S. Brewer, 1999

Byrne, Paula, 'Manners', in Janet Todd (ed.), *Jane Austen in Context*, Cambridge: Cambridge University Press, 2005, pp. 297–305

Copeland, Edward, 'Money', in Edward Copeland and Juliet McMaster (eds), *The Cambridge Companion to Jane Austen*, 2nd edn, Cambridge: Cambridge University Press, 2011, pp. 127–43

Dejardin, Kathleen, 'Etiquette and Marriage at the Turn of the 20th Century: Advice on Choosing One's Partner', in Jacques Carré (ed.), *The Crisis Of Courtesy: Studies in the Conduct Book in Britain, 1600–1900*, New York: E.J. Brill, 1994, pp. 167–79

Downing, Sarah Jane, *Fashion in the Time of Jane Austen*, Oxford: Shire Publications, 2010

Gay, Penny, 'Pastimes', in Janet Todd (ed.), *Jane Austen in Context*, Cambridge: Cambridge University Press, 2005, pp. 337–45

Girouard, Mark, *Life in the English Country House*, New Haven CT and London: Yale University Press, 1978

Kloester, Jennifer, *Georgette Heyer's Regency World: The Definitive Guide to the People, Places and Society in Georgette Heyer's Regency Novels*, London: William Heinemann, 2005

Lane, Maggie, 'Food', in Janet Todd (ed.), *Jane Austen in Context*, Cambridge: Cambridge University Press, 2005, pp. 262–8

Le Faye, Deirdre, *Jane Austen: The World of her Novels*, London: Francis Lincoln, 2002

McMaster, Juliet, 'Class', in Edward Copeland and Juliet McMaster (eds), *The Cambridge Companion to Jane* Austen, 2nd edn, Cambridge: Cambridge University Press, 2011, pp. 111–26

Murray, Venetia, *An Elegant Madness: High Society in Regency England*, London: Penguin Books, 1998

Pool, Daniel, *What Jane Austen Ate and Charles Dickens Knew: Fascinating Facts of Daily Life in the Nineteenth Century*, London: Robinson Publishing, 1998

Sullivan, Margaret C., *The Jane Austen Handbook: Proper Life Skills from Regency England*, Philadelphia PA: Quirk Books, 2007

Tannahill, Reay, *Food in History*, London: Penguin, 1988

Index